HOLY MACKEREL! DID Y

- why a false clue or a div...
  herring"?
- what "ham" has to do with overacting and amateur
  radio operators?
- how the lowly "nut" came to stand for both one's
  head and a man's gonads?

Christine Ammer, the cream of the crop of lexicographers, serves up the answers done to perfection. It's nourishment for the intellect—and delicious entertainment
too!

Christine Ammer, a graduate of Swarthmore College, is
the author of more than a dozen reference books on language, including *Southpaws and Sunday Punches, Have a
Nice Day—No Problem,* and *Seeing Red or Tickled Pink,* all
available in Plume books for Wordwatchers editions.

OTHER BOOKS BY CHRISTINE AMMER

fruitcakes & couch potatoes

And Other Delicious Expressions

Christine Ammer

A PLUME BOOK

PLUME
Published by the Penguin Group
Penguin Books USA Inc., 375 Hudson Street,
New York, New York 10014, U.S.A.
Penguin Books Ltd, 27 Wrights Lane, London W8 5TZ, England
Penguin Books Australia Ltd, Ringwood, Victoria, Australia
Penguin Books Canada Ltd, 10 Alcorn Avenue,
Toronto, Ontario, Canada M4V 3B2
Penguin Books (N.Z.) Ltd, 182–190 Wairau Road,
Auckland 10, New Zealand

Penguin Books Ltd, Registered Offices:
Harmondsworth, Middlesex, England

First published by Plume, an imprint of Dutton Signet,
a division of Penguin Books USA Inc.

First Printing, January, 1995
10 9 8 7 6 5 4 3 2 1

 REGISTERED TRADEMARK—MARCA REGISTRADA

LIBRARY OF CONGRESS CATALOGING IN PUBLICATION DATA
Ammer, Christine.
    Fruitcakes & couch potatoes, and other delicious expressions /
Christine Ammer.
        p.   cm.
    Includes index.
    ISBN 0-452-27368-4
    1. English language—Terms and phrases. 2. Dinners and dining—
Terminology. 3. English language—Etymology. 4. Gastonomy—Terminology.
5. Figures of speech. 6. Food—Terminology.   I. Title.
PE1689.A47   1995
422—dc20
                                                              94-19915
                                                              CIP

Printed in the United States of America
Set in Garamond no. 3
Designed by Eve L. Kirch

For Karen

CONTENTS

PREFACE

We not only are what we eat, but we talk about it all the time. Food-related terms and expressions abound—from *old chestnuts* like *cooking someone's goose* to calling our friends *fruitcakes* or *couch potatoes*.

The 1,000 or so terms in this book are arranged into thirteen categories, which cover the main kinds of food (fruits, vegetables, dairy products, meat, fish, etc.) and one final catchall for terms from dining and cooking. Within chapters the arrangement is roughly alphabetical, but readers seeking any particular term should consult the index at the back of the book.

Cross-references are indicated in small capital letters, for example, *see* FLESHPOTS in Chapter 8. Abbreviations are confined to one, the *OED,* for *Oxford English Dictionary,* that masterpiece of lexicography without which books like this one could never be attempted. Citations from the Bible identify chapter and verse, and from plays, the act and scene, in the conventional way of 1:2, where 1 represents chapter (or act) and 2 is the verse (or scene).

Warm thanks are due to the eminent lexicographers, ancient and modern, who have traced the origins of English, and to friends and family who have helped document usage and trace elusive terms. Bon appétit!

ONE

Food for Thought

The word *food* is generally defined as any nourishing substance that is taken into the body to sustain life, promote growth, or provide energy. It also may be characterized as solid and *edible,* as distinguished from *drink,* which is in liquid form. Or, as Ambrose Bierce defined *edible:* "Good to eat, and wholesome to digest, as a worm to a toad, a toad to a snake, a snake to a pig, a pig to a man, and a man to a worm." It may sound fanciful, but *food for worms* has for seven centuries been used for a dead human being, alluding to burial, decomposition, and eventually being fed on by earthworms. Similarly *food for fishes* has almost as long been applied to victims of drowning.

In earlier centuries the figurative uses of the word *food* ranged much farther afield, particularly in spiritual contexts. A fifteenth-century hymn to the Virgin described God as the singer's food, and Shakespeare used it as a metaphor for love ("My faire sonne, my life, my joy, my food . . ."). Later poets such as Cowper and Wordsworth had it in a more secular context, writing of food for the mind or intellect. From there it was but a short step to regarding an issue for discussion or consideration as *food for thought*, as Robert Southey had it in 1825: "A lively tale, and fraught/With food for thought" *(Tale of Paraguay;* cited by the *OED).*

TWO

Fruits of the Earth

The earliest human beings, like their simian forebears, survived by gathering whatever edible substances they could find in quantity. Raw fruits of various kinds were undoubtedly among the first human foodstuffs, and their value was recognized very early on, eons before the discovery of vitamin C and similar nutritional goodies.

In general a fruit is the part of a plant that contains its seeds, and a vegetable is any edible part of a plant. These definitions are not hard and fast, however, and both exceptions and overlaps abound. Peas and beans bear seeds and might be called fruits, but in fact they are generally called vegetables.

Moreover, both "vegetable" and "fruit" have additional and broader meanings. "Vegetable" often simply refers to any plant, in the widest sense. "Fruit," on the other hand, has the additional meaning of progeny or offspring (probably because it contains seeds) and, by extension, the outcome or product of something or someone. Both appear throughout the Bible. The *fruits of labor* appears over and over, beginning with Exodus 23:16: "The feast of harvest, the first fruits of thy labors." "Ye shall know them by their fruits," said the gospel writer (Matthew 7:16), and again, "By their fruits ye shall know them" (7:20). And the Catholic liturgy has it, "Hail Mary, blessed be the fruit of thy womb."

Among the more secular sources using "fruit" to mean "outcome" is the proverb, "Much bruit and little fruit," another way of saying, "A lot of talk but no results." It appears in Thomas Fuller's *The Holy Warre,* John Ray's *English Proverbs* (1670), and numerous other sources.

Further, fruit also acquired the connotation of wealth. When we speak of the *fruits of the earth* we are referring to natural riches, a meaning current since at least the fourteenth century. "The froytes of the erthe make plentuus," according to the author of *Lay Folks Mass Book* (c. 1375), and a similar sentiment appears in the *Book of Common Prayer,* "That it may please Thee to give and preserve to our use the kindly fruits of the earth."

Forbidden Fruit

Forbidden is fruit sweet.
—H. G. Bohn, *Handbook of Proverbs* (1855)

According to lexicographer Eric Partridge, *stolen fruit* is a metaphor for illicit love and alludes to the "apple" stolen by Eve in the Garden of Eden. That may be true, although nowhere is it stated that the Tree of Knowledge was one of carnal knowledge. Moreover, over the centuries it has been pointed out over and over that something forbidden or difficult to obtain has more appeal than something easily attainable. Ovid was but one who used fruit to express this thought: "It is more pleasing to pluck an apple from the branch which you have seized than to take one from a graven dish" *(Ex Ponto,* c. A.D. 13).

Nutty as a Fruitcake

For months they have lain in wait ... and now they are upon us, sodden with alcohol, their massive bodies bulging with strange green protuberances, attacking us in our homes ... at our offices—there is no escape, it is the hour of the fruitcake.
　　—Deborah Papier, "Yecch! The Dreaded Fruitcake," *Insight* (Dec. 23, 1985)

Oddly enough, the estimable *OED*'s first citation for "fruitcake, a cake containing fruit," is dated 1854. This type of cake, a heavy one containing fruit, especially raisins and other dried or candied fruits, was surely concocted long before that. Ideally, a fruitcake is made weeks or months in advance of consumption and is stored airtight to "cure," so as to develop maximum flavor.

In America fruitcakes became associated with Christmas, perhaps because of their similarity to the traditional British Yule confection called *plum pudding.* Not only are they served in households during the holiday season, but they often are presented as a Christmas gift. In fact, however, fruitcakes are not universally loved, although not everyone has so negative a reaction as that in the quotation above. Nevertheless, it is not uncommon for one recipient to pass the cake along as a gift to someone else, giving rise to many jokes about the wandering fruitcake.

Perhaps it is this dislike that gave rise to the colloquial use of *fruitcake* for a crazy or eccentric individual. More likely, however, is the fact that fruitcakes today usually contain nuts, and *nutty* has been used to mean "eccentric" since the late 1800s. G. and S. Lorimer had it in their *Heart Specialist* (1935), "Listen, Alix, you're as nutty as a fruitcake." More recently it appeared in Ann Landers's syndicated advice column: "It never fails—husbands who advertise they want sons always wind up nutty as fruitcakes over their daughters" *(Boston Globe,* Aug. 24, 1993). Here it is used in the sense of "crazy about," that is, passionately enthusiastic.

Being called a fruitcake is not usually complimentary, but it is nowhere near as disparaging or offensive as the use of *fruit* or *fruity* to describe male homosexuals. This slang usage became current in America in the 1940s but appears to have largely died out.

Finally, we have *fruit salad* (also known as *fruit cocktail* or *fruit cup),* a mélange of various cut-up fruits, fresh, canned, or frozen, served as an appetizer, side dish, or dessert. The colorful appearance of this mixture gave rise to the military slang use of *fruit salad* for two or more rows of military campaign ribbons decorating the breast of a uniform.

Apples

The apple, which is the most widely grown of all tree fruits and is produced in all moderate climates, has not escaped the problems of confusing nomenclature. The name *love-apple* was long used for the tomato, and not just in English—it was *pomme d'amour* in French and *Liebesapfel* in German. And the name *earth-apple* was used for the potato, which is still called *pomme de terre* in modern French and *Erdapfel* in colloquial German.

But of the tree of knowledge of good and evil, thou shalt not eat of it.

—Genesis 2:17

Apples are eaten all over the world in various guises—raw, stewed, baked, and roasted, in applesauce, apple juice and cider, apple jelly, and apple butter. Among the most familiar stories involving apples is that about Adam and Eve in the Garden of Eden, where Eve succumbs to temptation and eats some forbidden fruit. Today most people think of this fruit as an apple, but in fact nowhere in the Bible is the fruit identified specifically. According to Muslim belief, it was a banyan or Indian fig. Only later did Jewish and Christian tradition invariably make it an apple. (Some scholars believe that this identification came via readers of the Latin translation, the Vulgate Bible, and is based on the similarity between the Latin *malus* for "bad" and *malum* for "apple.")

In any event, apple has stuck, and in more ways than one: the familiar name *Adam's apple* was based on the idea that this projection of the thyroid cartilage at the front of the neck, which is more prominent in men than in women, was "caused" by Adam's eating a piece of the famous apple that got stuck in his throat.

The Apple of His Eye

The ancient Hebrews were partial to apples in naming a number of body parts. They used them for kneecaps, for tonsils, and for the heads of bones, as well as for the eye's pupil, called *the apple of the eye*. This expression very quickly was transferred to mean any object or person very dear to one— after all, eyes are precious indeed. In the Bible it first crops up as "He kept him as the apple of his eye," referring to God's cherishing Israel (Deuteronomy 32:10), and reappears in at least two other Old Testament books, Proverbs (7:2) and Psalms (17:8).

The Apples of Sodom

The ancient Hebrew city of Sodom was destroyed along with Gomorrah for its wickedness, according to chapters 18 and 19 of the Book of Genesis, and gave rise to the word *sodomy* for sexual practices frowned on if not forbidden in the late Middle Ages. The *apples of Sodom* have a similar negative meaning. They are a yellow fruit that grows on the shores of the Dead Sea, beautiful to look at but extremely bitter to taste and filled with tiny black seeds that resemble ashes. Consequently they became a metaphor for extreme disappointment. John de Trevisa wrote of them in 1398: "Ther [by the Dead Sea] groweth most feyre applis . . . and when thou takest, he fadeth and falleth in to ashes." Poets continued to mention them over the centuries, as Byron did in his *Childe Harold,* but the term is heard less often today. A similar sentiment is expressed in an ancient proverb, cited as long ago as 1275 by the unknown collector of the *Proverbs of Alfred:* "Mani appel is uten grene briht on beme and biter with-innen" (Many an apple is fair on the tree and bitter within).

The Apple of Discord

Apples figured in ancient Greek legend as well. Among the most famous is the *apple of discord,* which in modern terminology still means a cause of dispute. At the wedding of Thetis and Peleus, where all the gods and goddesses were assembled, Eris (Discord), furious that she had not been invited, threw among them a golden apple inscribed "for the fairest of them all." Three of the goddesses claimed it as their own—Hera (Juno), Pallas Athena (Minerva), and Aphrodite (Venus). Each tried to bribe Paris, who was to decide which should have it, Hera promising him power and wealth, Pallas Athena military victory, and Aphrodite possession of the most beautiful woman on earth. He chose Aphrodite, who then helped him to seduce Helen of Troy, setting off the Trojan Wars, and the vengeance of the other two goddesses was said to have caused the fall of Troy.

Golden apples figure in several other Greek legends as well as in Scandinavian mythology, where Iduna guarded golden apples tasted by the gods when they wished to renew their youth. She was lured away from her post by the evil Loki, but eventually was restored, so that the gods could grow young again and spring could return to the earth.

The term *apple-cheeked* appears often in Homer's *Iliad* and *Odyssey,* where it originally meant blushing. Since the early nineteenth century, however, it has been used merely to describe a healthy, ruddy complexion, particularly in youngsters.

William Tell and Isaac Newton

Apples figure in later legends as well. In the thirteenth century the Swiss patriot William Tell defied Gessler, steward of the Austrian duke, Albert I, and as punishment was told to shoot with his bow and arrow an apple placed on his own son's head. Tell succeeded without harming the boy and later killed Gessler. In the uprising that followed, Switzerland won independence from the hated Hapsburgs.

This story is almost certainly pure invention but became so popular that it was repeated by numerous chroniclers, including Friedrich von Schiller, who transformed it into a popular play, *William Tell* (1809), and Gioacchino Rossini, who used it as the subject of his last opera (1829).

Another oft-repeated apple legend is the story of Sir Isaac Newton, which was told (and perhaps originated) by the French philosopher Voltaire. Allegedly Newton's niece told Voltaire that while the British physicist was visiting his mother in 1666, he saw an apple fall from a tree. It was this everyday occurrence that supposedly led him to formulate his laws of gravitation and laws of motion, the two achievements for which he is best remembered.

An Apple a Day

Ascribing medicinal value to apples dates from the sixteenth century. "An apple a day keeps the doctor away" is the more or less straight modern version, but numerous others exist. In the *Arabian Nights,* Prince Ahmed buys an apple at Samarkand that is said to cure all diseases. "He that will not a wife wed must eat a cold apple when he goeth to bed," wrote Thomas Cogan, author of *The Haven of Health* (1612), referring to the belief that an apple quenches "the flame of Venus" (that is, sexual desire). The same sentiment, if not precisely the same idea, was echoed by E. M. Wright in *Rustic Speech* (1913), "Ait a happle avore gwain to bed, An' you'll make the doctor beg his bread." And probably both were meant by the humorist who quipped, "An apple a day keeps the doctor away, as the lover of the doctor's wife said when he urged her to feed her husband apples."

The Rotten Apple

The rotten apple spoils his companion.
—Benjamin Franklin, *Poor Richard's Almanack* (1736)

The contagiousness of rotten apples was observed long before the mechanism of such spoilage was understood. It is documented in an ancient Latin proverb, *Pomum compunctum cito corrumpit sibi iunctum,* which was translated into English by Dan Michel of Northgate (in *Ayenbite of Inwyt,* 1340) and cited by Chaucer in *The Cokes Tale.*

No amount of polishing will restore a rotten apple to health, as any *wise apple* will tell any *apple polisher.* The term *wise apple,* for a clever, shrewd individual, is generally thought to be a variant of "wiseacre," meaning the same thing. However, John Ciardi discovered that a particular variety of apple was so called in England because it blooms so late that it misses the spring frosts (and the attendant risk of losing its blossoms, and consequently fruit).

The term *apple polishing* for attempting to win someone's favor through flattery and gifts comes from the practice of schoolchildren bringing the gift of a bright, shiny apple to their teacher (in hopes of better grades or some other form of tutorial mercy). An Americanism, it has been around since the 1920s or perhaps even longer. Only slightly older is *apple-knocker,* derogatory American slang for a farm worker since about 1910; it alludes to the practice of picking apples by knocking them down from the tree.

Upset the Applecart

A much older locution is to *upset the applecart,* which has been around since ancient Roman times, although occasionally with somewhat different meanings. The Roman writer Plautus used it c. 200 B.C., *"Plaustrum perculi,"* translated as "I've upset the cart" and meaning "I've ruined things." This is the most common usage, but the estimable Francis Grose, in his *Dictionary of the Vulgar Tongue* (1796), held that the cart, which had become an applecart by this time, really stood for the human body, and upsetting it meant knocking someone down. Nevertheless, other late eighteenth-century citations point to the more common and present-day use of the term, as, for example, by J. Belknap in 1788, "S[amuel] Adams had almost overset the apple-cart by intruding an amendment of his own fabrication on the morning of the day of ratification [of the Constitution]" (cited by the *OED*).

Apple-Pie Order

> *"Apple-pie order,"* said Mr. Boffin.
> —Charles Dickens, *Our Mutual Friend* (1865)

Although pastry chefs and good home cooks alike may pride themselves on neatly arranging apple slices on a pie crust, this term for meticulous neatness most likely has a quite different source, and nothing whatever to do with apples. It apparently is a British corruption of the French phrase, *nappes pliées en ordre,* meaning linen neatly folded.

Some authorities believe that the same phrase also is the source of *apple-pie bed,* referring to the venerable boarding-school and summer-camp trick of doubling back the bottom sheet so that a person getting into bed cannot extend his or her legs very far. However, in the author's checkered childhood this practice of short-sheeting was simply called making a *pie-bed,* and both these terms probably allude to folding over a turnover or similar piecrust pastry. This theory is verified by Francis Grose, who defined it, "A bed made apple-pye fashion, like what is called a turnover apple-pye, where the sheets are so doubled as to prevent anyone from getting at his length between them; a common trick played by frolicsome country lasses on their sweethearts, male relations, or visitors" (1796).

As American as apple pie is a puzzling term, inasmuch as apple pies were being baked in England long before America was colonized. Nevertheless, apple pie has been identified with American patriotism, family values, community spirit, and similar virtues often addressed in political speeches for a very long time. As William Zinsser put it when discussing hot dogs, "we have long since made it [the hot dog] our own, a twin pillar of democracy along with Mom's apple pie. In fact, now that Mom's apple pie comes frozen and baked by somebody who isn't Mom, the hot dog stands alone" *(Life,* Oct. 9, 1969).

The Big Apple

> *Do that stomp with lots of pomp and romance,*
> *Big Apple, big apple!*
> —Lee David and John Redmond,
> "The Big Apple" (1937)

Present-day fans and promoters of New York City's pleasures often refer to that metropolis as "the Big Apple." Actually, this contemporary-sounding term was born in the early twentieth century and originally was a metaphor for any big city. By the early 1920s it was being extended to the peak of certain endeavors—Broadway, a top jazz club, competing for big bucks at a New York racetrack. Finally it became a nickname for New York City, kept alive mainly by jazz musicians who, if they played in New York, believed they were now in "the big time." (One source suggests there was a Harlem nightclub known as the Big Apple that jazz musicians held in high regard.) In the swing era of the late 1930s the Big Apple was the name of a popular dance. It was described, in a song of the same name by Lee David and John Redmond, as a round dance. The dancers formed a circle and a caller shouted out the movements, which actually combined various steps from such earlier dances as the shag and black bottom. Both the song and the dance, which ended with shouting the words "Praise Allah!" have largely died out, but the Big Apple is still very much alive. (John Ciardi suggests the term was originally a translation of the Spanish *manzana principal, manzana* meaning both apple and city block, and holds it was first used by black jazz musicians in New Orleans about 1910, but this origin seems unlikely.) In the 1970s the New York City Convention Bureau adopted Big Apple as a nickname for the city, replacing the earlier name Fun City.

Apples and Oranges

Another twentieth-century term is *apples and oranges,* used as a metaphor for dissimilarity. For example, "You can't compare a huge conglomerate to a small family-owned enterprise; that's comparing apples and oranges." Its origin is no longer known, but some speculate it comes from arithmetic lessons teaching youngsters that one cannot add unlike objects. In any event, it has totally replaced the much older *apples and oysters,* which dates from the sixteenth century and appeared as a proverb in John Ray's 1670 collection. "No more like than an apple to an oyster," declared Sir Thomas More *(Works,* 1557). Thomas Fuller's *Gnomologia* of 1732 introduced apples and lobsters, but that did not become particularly common. And Cockney rhyming slang has *apples and pears* for "stairs," but this phrase has nothing to do with disparity.

Applesauce

I wasn't born yesterday, and I know apple sauce when I hear it.
—Ring Lardner, *Zone of Quiet* (1926)

The name "applesauce" for a purée of stewed apples sweetened with sugar has been around since the early eighteenth century, and the dish probably much longer than that. Its transfer to mean nonsense, or wild exaggeration, or insincere flattery, dates from the early 1920s and began in America. It is less often heard today.

Bananas

A tropical fruit, the banana probably originated in southern Asia and has been known in the Western world since ancient times. Alexander the Great found it in India in 327 B.C.

Banana Republic

Bananas began to be imported into the United States in the first half of the nineteenth century, mainly from Cuba. By 1900 they constituted a tremendous trade in Latin America, largely sponsored by U.S. businesses that set up railroads and shipping lines to transport the fruit (in *banana boats*) from Costa Rica, Guatemala, El Salvador, and other Latin American countries. Those nations, whose economy now depended largely on this fruit, began to be called, in the 1930s, *banana republics,* a term today considered disparaging and demeaning. (No such pejorative sense attaches to *Bananaland,* a colloquial Australian name for the state of Queensland, where bananas also grow.) A 1971 film, *Bananas,* by Woody Allen, is a hilarious treatment of a revolution in just such a country. However, the farce does not mitigate the unfortunate truth that the former banana republics have had serious economic problems and a difficult and often violent political history.

> *It's all the same whether up or down*
> *You slip on a peel of banana brown.*
> —Ambrose Bierce, *The Devil's Dictionary* (1881–1906)

The humor in Allen's movie is often of the *banana-peel variety*—that is, broad farce. The term alludes to a pratfall caused by slipping on a banana peel, a comic device dating from the early 1900s. Eric Partridge also chronicled the catch phrase, "You've got one foot in the grave and the other on a banana skin," meaning you're in a very precarious position, which he said was common in British soccer clubs in the 1920s.

The banana crops up in a number of specialized sports terms that generally allude to its physical properties (curved and soft). In soccer a *banana kick* denotes an off-center kick that makes the ball curve or bend in flight before suddenly dropping, and in golf a *banana ball* is a sliced ball that travels in a long arc. In ice hockey a *banana blade* is a stick with an exaggeratedly curved blade, affording the player better leverage (but there are rules governing the maximum curve allowed). In baseball a *banana stick* is a poorly made bat, which is in effect too soft. Finally, the *banana seat* of a bicycle is tapered at the front and curves upward at the back.

Show business, initially vaudeville and later legitimate theater, used the term *top banana* for the leading comedian in a show, probably beginning in the early twentieth century but not cited by conventional sources until about 1950. (It may first have been used for Frank Lebowitz, a burlesque comedian who used bananas in his act.) This in turn gave rise to *second banana* for a supporting comedian. Both terms have been transferred to more general usage, top banana to the principal individual in any group or undertaking and, somewhat less often, second banana to a supporting person.

An older but still current usage is that of *bananas* to mean crazy in an excited or violent fashion, particularly in the phrases *to go bananas* and *to drive (someone) bananas.* John Ciardi theorized that the analogy here is to the banana's being curved (rather than straight) but offers no verification, and he dated it from about 1900. The earliest citation in the *OED,* however, is dated 1935, and the *American Speech* editors find one only in 1957.

Yes, We Have No Bananas

The use of *banana oil,* a paint solvent and artificial-flavor agent, for nonsense or gibberish dates from the 1920s. The analogy here is unclear, if ever there was one, and the term appears to be dying out, at least in America. This is not true of an equally meaningless expression, *Yes, we have no bananas,* which according to Eric Partridge was one of *the* most popular catch phrases of the 1920s. It began as the title and refrain of a highly popular nonsense song by Frank Silver and Irving Cohn—"Yes, we have no bananas, we have no bananas today"—who allegedly got the idea by overhearing a Greek fruit peddler tell a customer, "Yes, we have no bananas." According to popular-song authority David Ewen, they introduced the song in a New York restaurant, but it failed to catch on. In 1923, however, Eddie Cantor saw the song in manuscript while a revue he was starring in, *Make It Snappy,* was playing in Philadelphia. Held over for an extended run, the show needed new material, since patrons were coming to see it a second time. Cantor decided to include "Yes, We Have No Bananas" in one of his routines, and the song stopped the show for more than a quarter of an hour. The song was retained, of course, and Cantor continued to bring down the house with it. By the end of the year it was being sung all over America. Subsequent revivals helped keep the phrase alive. In 1930 the song was used in the motion-picture musical *Mammy,* starring Al Jolson, and in 1954 Eddie Cantor sang it on the soundtrack of *The Eddie Cantor Story.* Perhaps the greatest tribute to the song came from humorist Will Rogers, who in a piece entitled "The Greatest Document in American Literature" (1924) wrote, "The subject for this brainy Editorial is resolved that, 'Is the Song Yes We Have No Bananas the greatest or the worst Song that America ever had?' " and concludes, "I would rather have been the Author of that Banana Masterpiece than the Author of the Constitution of the United States. No one has offered any amendments to it. It's the only thing ever written in America that we haven't changed, most of them for the worst." And, of course, the phrase as it stands is utter nonsense.

It's the Berries

Generally speaking, a berry is a small, juicy fruit, roughly round in shape and usually stoneless. Among the best-known

kinds are blackberries, blueberries and huckleberries, currants, gooseberries, mulberries, raspberries, and strawberries.

In early twentieth-century American slang, *the berries* meant superlative or outstanding. "It's the berries" was more or less equivalent to the roughly contemporary "it's the cat's pajamas," but like the latter is no longer heard.

Although blackberries both grow wild and are cultivated in America, linguistically they are better known in Great Britain. They are apparently prolific, whence the term *plentiful as black-berries,* used (and perhaps invented) by Shakespeare *(Henry IV,* Part 1, 2:4). The British equivalent of America's Indian summer—a spell of warm, sunny weather in late September and early October—is *blackberry summer,* since that is the time of the berry harvest.

Blueberries also are known on both sides of the Atlantic, but it is the name of a native American variety, the *huckleberry,* that crops up most frequently. They, too, are prolific, and *thick as huckleberries* was a common simile by the 1830s. The berry turns up in several comparative contexts as well, where it generally means a small amount or slightly. *"Within a huckleberry* [emphasis added] of being smothered to death" (J. K. Paulding, *Westward Ho,* 1832)—that is, very close to being smothered—is one of the earliest. It was still current in 1920, when Edward Bok wrote, "He always kept 'a huckleberry or two' ahead of his readers" *(Americanization).* A more curious comparison is one that turns up throughout the nineteenth century. "It's a disgraceful shot—what I call a full *huckleberry below a persimmon* [emphasis added]," wrote J. K. Paulding *(Banks of the Ohio,* 1833). And similarly, although in the opposite direction, "I'm a huckleberry above that persimmon because I'm the chief cook" (D. A. Porter, *Incidents of the Civil War,* 1885). Both phrases allude to the disparate size of the plants, that is, the low-growing huckleberry bush versus the much taller (thirty to sixty feet high) persimmon tree. (Also see PERSIMMONS below.)

The huckleberry also functioned like the twentieth-century raspberry (see below). "He *got the huckleberry* [emphasis added], as we used to say in college," wrote Henry A. Beers *(Century Magazine,* 1883), meaning he was derided. Further, it denoted romantic suitability, as in "If she were looking for a husband, you were her huckleberry." Both usages are obsolete.

Undoubtedly the best-known huckleberry in history is *Huckleberry Finn,* the hero of Mark Twain's novel *The Adventures of Huckleberry Finn* (1884). He first appeared in Twain's *The Adventures of Tom Sawyer* (1875), where he is described as the juvenile pariah of the village, son of the town drunkard, neglected, ragged, and often hungry, but, to the envy of respectable children, free from rules, church or school attendance, bathing, and similar restrictions. His name is never explained, but possibly it relates to the meaning of huckleberry as a trifle, something of little worth, which was how Huck Finn was considered by the townspeople. If this allusion accounts for Twain's choice of his name, it is ironic, since royalties from these two books were far from trifling, making the author very wealthy indeed.

In the late 1950s, *Huckleberry Hound* became a well-known character in a television cartoon show of that name by Hanna-Barbera, which also introduced the even more popular Yogi Bear. However, it is doubtful that he will achieve the lasting fame of Twain's Huck Finn.

The *gooseberry* is better known in Britain than in America, as are most of the terms concerning it. "All the other gifts are *not worth a gooseberry,*" wrote Shakespeare in *Henry IV* (Part 2, 1:2), implying both small size and little worth. To *play gooseberry* in the nineteenth century meant to chaperone lovers. Dr. Ebenezer Brewer speculated that this phrase refers to a tactful chaperon going off to pick gooseberries so as to give the lovers privacy. On the other hand, to *play old gooseberry* with something or someone meant to make havoc or take great liberties. It may also be obsolete.

The *mulberry* also is better known in the Old World than the New. One variety of mulberry bears red berries, and legend has it that they were originally white but became blood-red from the blood of Pyramus and Thisbe. However, the black or American mulberry bears dark, purplish-red berries, giving rise to the adjective *mulberry-faced* for someone very red in the face. Tennyson had it in *Lucretius:*

> Hired animalisms, vile as though that made
> The mulberry-faced Dictator's orgie worse
> Than aught they fable of the quiet Gods.

While this term is seldom heard in America, *Here we go round the mulberry bush* remains a popular children's game on both sides of the Atlantic. The children stand in a circle and act out the words to the song, at first walking in a circle (Here we go round . . .), then pretending to wash clothes (This is the way we wash our clothes . . .), etc. And, alluding to their clusterlike habit of growth, dentists call a tooth with more than the usual four cusps a *mulberry molar.*

To *give someone the raspberry* means to show extreme disrespect by making a rude noise with the tongue pushed through the lips. It has been so called since the nineteenth century, and the *Random House Unabridged Dictionary* (second edition) advances the theory that it originated as a shortening of "raspberry tart," rhyming slang for "fart" (for the sound produced) but gives no conclusive evidence for it.

Strawberries

> *Casey would waltz with the strawberry blonde,*
> *And the band played on.*
> —John E. Palmer (words) and Charles B. Ward (music),
>   "The Band Played On" (1895)

Strawberries are singularly appealing to the human palate. "Doubtless God could have made a better berry, but doubtless God never did," wrote Dr. William Butler about 1621, a statement with which Izaak Walton (of *The Compleat Angler*) and numerous later writers concurred. The annual world-famous tennis tournament held at Wimbledon, England, is every bit as renowned for the strawberries and cream served there as for its championship. And all this despite the fact that "One man's strawberries, another man's hives," as some humorist quipped—for strawberries are among the items frequently involved in food allergy.

The *strawberry blonde* in the Gay Nineties song quoted above has hair of an attractive, reddish-blond color. The raised, bright red, berry-like birthmark called a *strawberry mark* is not considered particularly beautiful. Technically called a capillary hemangioma, it develops soon after birth and tends to enlarge slowly over the next few months. In the majority of cases it will disappear by itself within five to seven years. Those that do not are either left or treated with medication. This birthmark figures in a famous nineteenth-century farce, J. M. Morton's *Box and Cox,* about two lodgers who, each unknown to the other, alternately occupy the same boardinghouse room, one at night and the other by day. When they finally meet, a distinctive strawberry mark present on one enables them to recognize each other as long-lost brothers.

Life Is Just a Bowl of Cherries

Cherries, which may have originated in China some four thousand years ago, were first cultivated in Greece. They were introduced to America with the earliest settlers, and the trees were well established before the American Revolution—as witnessed by the famous legend of young George Washington's hatchet attack on his father's favorite tree. Japanese cherry trees, grown only for their beautiful blossoms (their fruit doesn't amount to much), are a mecca for tourists in Washington, D.C., every spring; the capital's trees were a gift from the city of Tokyo.

Cherries, like many fruits, must be picked by hand to avoid being damaged. Thus the well-known *cherry picker* is something of a misnomer. It actually is a crane with a movable boom, enabling a worker at the top to pick fruit, or, more commonly, repair telephone lines, prune trees, and do similar chores. The term has been used for such devices only since the first half of the twentieth century. In the 1800s, however, it became a nickname for the 11th Hussars when a detachment of theirs was surprised by French cavalry in a Spanish orchard in 1811 and had to fight a dismounted action. They also were called *Cherry Breeches* and *Cherrybums* for the very tight red trousers their officers were commanded to wear in 1840 by their regimental commander, the seventh Earl of Cardigan. This usage died out, along with the regiment (they merged with another to form the Royal Hussars in 1969). In twentieth-century basketball, *to cherry pick* means to remain near the basket while play is at the other end of the court, in hopes of receiving a long pass and making an easy (because it is undefended) basket.

Another twentieth-century term is *cherry bomb,* which has no ballistic significance but alludes only to the fruit's appearance: it is a red, globe-shaped firecracker that explodes with a loud bang. It has been so called since about 1950.

A number of sayings about cherries allude to their small size, sometimes (but not always) equated with little worth. Thus, something *not worth a cherry* has meant, since the fifteenth century, practically worthless. On the other hand, the use of *cherry* for virginity, or the hymen, a rather vulgar colloquialism used since the mid-nineteenth century, does not necessarily imply lack of worth. It in turn gave rise to the adjectival use of *cherry* for new or unused

(as in "This bike's in cherry condition") and also for inexperienced.

Cherries figure in a number of old proverbs, some obvious and others cryptic. "A cherry year, a merry year," in John Ray's proverb collection of 1678, makes reasonably good sense. Cherry blossoms are pretty to look at, and a good harvest is always a good thing. More puzzling is the addition of "A Plumb year, a dumb year," which appeared in Thomas Fuller's *Gnomologia* (1732). Cherries are closely related to plums—both belong to the botanical genus *Prunus*—but why a dumb year? Perhaps it is only the rhyme that appealed. On the other hand, "Never make two bites at a cherry—take it all" seems eminently sensible. It means don't divide something that's too small to be divided, and has been around since at least the sixteenth century.

Perhaps the most bizarre cautionary proverb is, "He that eateth cherries with noblemen shall have his eyes squirted out with the stones," which first appeared in Randle Cotgrave's *Dictionary* of 1611 and was repeated in numerous later collections. Happily, its meaning has been lost and its dictate forgotten.

As for *life is just a bowl of cherries,* this phrase began life as the title of a song with words by Lew Brown and music by Ray Henderson, introduced in 1931 and popularized by Ethel Merman. Originally it expressed a very optimistic outlook—that is, life is simply wonderful—but as a catch phrase it came to be used ironically. The humor writer Erma Bombeck punned on it in the title of her book, *If Life Is a Bowl of Cherries, What Am I Doing in the Pits?* (1978), "pits" here alluding to both cherry pits and the nadir of any circumstances.

In bowling jargon a *cherry* denotes knocking down a front pin in such a way that it misses other pins of a relatively easy lie. No bowler would want a bowl of these cherries.

Citrus Fruits

The word *citrus* is actually the Latin name of the citrus tree, which bears a lemon-colored, thick-rinded fruit, larger than the lemon. Today mainly the rinds of the fruit are used in candied or preserved form, but the name itself was given to the botanical genus that also includes grapefruit, lemons, limes, and oranges, as well as the somewhat less familiar pomelo or shaddock, tangelo, and tangerine. All of these fruits contain *citric acid,* a sharp-tasting colorless substance so called since about 1800. And nearly all of their names have been transferred in one way or another. The most frequent transfer alludes to the color of their skin: *orange* and *tangerine* are actually the names of colors, and *lemon yellow* and *lime green* similarly call up specific shades.

Grapefruit, Lemons, Limes

The *grapefruit,* which is at least a partial misnomer since it is in no way related to grapes—the name dates from the early 1800s and presumably refers to its clusterlike habit of growth—has given its name to the *Grapefruit League.* An Americanism, this name denotes those major-league baseball teams that go for spring training to Florida, a major producer of grapefruit. Warm spring weather occurs much earlier there than in their home cities (Boston, Toronto, etc.), and this term differentiates them from teams that do their spring training in the similarly warmer climate of Arizona.

Lemons are among the most sour of the citrus fruits, and presumably this quality has caused their name to be transferred in negative contexts. In mid-nineteenth-century Britain a *lemon* was a person with a tart disposition, which later was extended to a caustic or sarcastic remark. In later nineteenth-century slang the term was used for a person easily duped, that is, a sucker. In twentieth-century U.S. terminology, however, a *lemon* became an object that was defective or otherwise disappointing. In the second half of the century it was particularly often applied to a defective automobile, and in the 1980s numerous states passed *lemon laws* to protect consumers against defects; they required the manufacturer and/or seller of a defective car to repair or replace it, or refund the buyer's money.

Limes are at least as sour as lemons, but the principal transfer of their name was to British seamen, called *Limeys* because on long voyages they were given lime juice to prevent scurvy (a vitamin C deficiency disease). In Australia, the United States, Canada, and other English-speaking nations, this name was later transferred to any British individual, often but not always in a disparaging sense.

Oranges and Lemons
Say the Bells of St. Clements.

This old church-bell chant of British children probably referred to the bells of St. Clement in Eastcheap, near the London wharves where cargoes of citrus fruit used to be unloaded. However, it was adopted by a different London church, St. Clement Danes in the Strand, which since 1920, after its famous bells were restored, has held an annual Oranges and Lemons service. It is attended by the pupils of the nearby primary school, who play the "Oranges and Lemons" tune on handbells and then each receives an orange and a lemon.

Oranges

Of all the citrus fruits, oranges are linguistically the most interesting. Beginning with Shakespeare's *"civil as an orange, and something of that jealous complexion" (Much Ado About Nothing,* 2:1), it has cropped up again and again. A swelling that stretches the skin so much that pores become visible is called *peau d'orange,* French for "orange skin."

Orange juice was apparently valued from early times. An orange squeezed dry was a frequent metaphor for discarding something or someone no longer useful. Baltasar Gracian had it in *The Courtier's Oracle* (1685), and Frederick the Great repeated it with reference to Voltaire's serving him for only one more year (1751). It also denoted something completely used up. Ralph Waldo Emerson, in his essay *Conduct of Life: Culture* (1860), said of the city, "New York is a sucked orange." James M. Dixon personalized it: "He was a sucked orange; his brain was dry" *(Dictionary of Idiomatic Phrases,* 1891).

The orange tree is extremely prolific, and it therefore came to symbolize fruitfulness. The white (for virginity) orange blossom therefore became a conventional bridal decoration, and the saying *to go gathering orange blossoms* meant to go looking for a wife.

The most curious transfer of orange was made in the 1950s, *queer as a clockwork orange,* a Cockney slang term applied to British homosexuals in the 1950s. The image of a mechanism (clockwork) inserted into an organism (orange fruit) caught the imagination of Anthony Burgess, who used it as the title of his 1962 novel about a brainwashed individual. It was later made into a popular motion picture, which helped this strange term to survive.

The thin outer peel of oranges and other citrus fruits has a stronger, more piquant flavor than the fruit itself and has long been used to spice up various foods and beverages. In cookbooks this peel is called *zest,* a word taken directly from the French name for such peels in the seventeenth century (today the French is spelled *zeste)* and eventually extended to figurative use. Today zest means not only citrus peel but, primarily, hearty enjoyment, keen relish, or lively energy—all senses derived from the original flavorful peel.

Coconut

> *Your cocoa is very near a sledgehammer. If it isn't hard, it may get cracked.*
>
> —J. C. Neal, *Charcoal Sketches* (1837)

The fruit of the tropical coconut palm was introduced to Europeans in the sixteenth century and became linguistically enshrined in a number of sayings. The fruit's outstanding characteristics, roundness and hardness, were transferred to the human cranium—that is, *coconut,* sometimes spelled *cocoanut,* and the shortened *cocoa* became slang words for head, particularly in America (see the quotation above).

In late nineteenth-century Britain, *Give the gentleman a coconut!* and *Everyone a coconut!* were shouted by fairgrounds barkers to attract customers to the *coconut shy,* a kind of shooting gallery where one tried to knock down coconuts by throwing a ball at them. The reward for succeeding was a coconut. Presumably it is this attraction that is referred to in Fred Heatherton's 1948 song:

> *I've got a loverly bunch of coconuts,*
> *There they are a-standing in a row,*
> *Big ones, small ones, some as big as your head . . .*

In Britain both of these phrases subsequently were transferred to other undertakings, the first to any successful effort (Give her a coconut, i.e., she wins) and the second to a series of successes (Everyone a coconut, i.e., all his plays are Broadway hits).

A catch phrase that originated in mid-nineteenth-century America is *So that accounts for the milk in the coconut,* meaning, "So that's the explanation for some puzzling item or circumstance." It soon crossed the Atlantic and was widespread for a time but is not often heard today.

In the twentieth century the coconut achieved notoriety of a far less happy sort in 1942, when a fire broke out in Boston's *Cocoanut Grove* nightclub, so named for its tropical décor. The exit doors in that establishment opened inward, and in the resulting panic nearly five hundred persons died. It remains one of the worst fire disasters in history.

Not Worth a Fig

I wouldn't give a fig for the pair.
—Aristophanes, *The Peace* (421 B.C.)

The fig is one of the oldest cultivated fruits, nutritious and easy to preserve by drying, a staple food of ancient peoples in southern Arabia and southern Europe. Nevertheless, it has been equated with worthlessness since ancient times. Aristophanes' contemptuous statement was echoed by Plautus, Rabelais, Erasmus, Shakespeare, Jonathan Swift, and O. Henry, to name just a few writers. Spoken aloud, it often was accompanied by an insulting gesture, either a snap of the fingers or the even ruder insertion of the thumb between index and middle finger, and the gestures themselves came to be called "making a fig" (in Dante's Italian, *far le fiche;* in La Fontaine's French, *faire la figue;* in Shakespearean language, *the Fig of Spain*).

According to the Bible, figs grew in the Garden of Eden, for it was *fig leaves* that Adam and Eve used to cover the nakedness they became aware of only after eating the forbidden fruit (Genesis 3:7). In subsequent eras, periodic attacks of modesty made sculptors and painters cover the genitals of naked figures with representations of fig-leaf aprons, more or less stylized. The term *fig leaf* also is occasionally transferred to anything intended to hide something indecorous or indecent. (However, the expressions *in full fig* and *in fine fig,* used from about the mid-seventeenth century to mean "dressed up" and "in excellent condition," have nothing to do with the fig or its leaves but are variants of the obsolete word *feague* and the Germanic *fegen,* to polish.)

Finally, *Fig Sunday* is an old dialect name for Palm Sunday, when figs are eaten to commemorate Jesus's cursing a barren fig tree and causing it to wither.

Grapes of Wrath

Mine eyes have seen the glory of the
coming of the Lord,
He has trampled out the vintage where
the grapes of wrath are stored.
                              —Julia Ward Howe, "Battle Hymn
                              of the Republic" (1862)

The cultivation of grapes dates so far back in antiquity that it is not known where they originated. The Bible, which is the source of perhaps the two best-known metaphors, *grapes of*

wrath and *sour grapes,* speaks of grape cultivation in the time of
Noah. Grape seeds have been found in Swiss lake dwellings
from the Bronze Age, and the first European visitors to North
America, the Norsemen, found grape vines so abundant there
that they called the newfound continent Vinland.

Although we associate *sour grapes* with Aesop's fable about
the fox that, unable to reach some grapes, dismissed them as
sour, the actual phrase if not the precise metaphor for putting
down the unattainable is even older. The Old Testament books
of Ezekiel and Jeremiah, which antedate Aesop, have, "The fathers have eaten sour grapes, and the children's teeth are set on
edge." Today, however, the term nearly always takes on Aesop's
meaning, as in, "Many of these anonymous critics, of course,
had wanted the job for themselves. . . . These stories contained
enough sour grapes to fill a vineyard" (Bob Kuttner, *Boston
Globe,* January 8, 1993).

The grapes of wrath in Julia Ward Howe's famous Civil
War song, sung to the melody of "John Brown's Body" at war
rallies, in army camps, on battlefields, and on such state occasions as Lyndon Johnson's presidential inauguration and Winston Churchill's funeral (both in 1965), come from the New

Testament book of Revelation: "And the angel ... gathered the vine of the earth, and cast it into the great winepress of the wrath of God." John Steinbeck adopted it as the title of his 1939 novel dramatizing the plight of dispossessed Okies (Oklahomans) forced to leave the Dust Bowl of their foreclosed fields and farms for an uncertain future in the West.

The grape extolled by poets generally means wine rather than the fruit. A number of things resembling grapes in appearance have been given their name, among them the *grape hyacinth,* a spring-blooming bulb bearing a cluster of globular flowers resembling a bunch of grapes; *grapes,* a form of tuberculosis in cattle and horses characterized by the internal formation of grapelike clusters; and *grapeshot,* a cluster of small cast-iron balls formerly used in cannons. The last, although obviously obsolete, became famous through its use by Thomas Carlyle in *The French Revolution* (1837). He described the ease with which Napoleon's artillery put down the Paris Rebellion of 1795 as a "whiff of grapeshot."

The *grapevine,* although its origin may be forgotten, is far from obsolete. This name for an informal system of rumor spreading comes from a *grapevine telegraph* used by Abolitionists who helped slaves escape. They would string a clothesline to signal either danger or safety, according to what was hung on it, and since rope was costly, grapevines were sometimes substituted for it. During the Civil War wires were strung along trees to facilitate military communications, but the name stuck, perhaps because when such wires became loosened they trailed on the ground in the manner of wild grapevines; further, it became associated with less than accurate information. Long after more sophisticated methods replaced the actual grapevine telegraph, the name was retained with its present meaning.

Melon

Men and melons are hard to know.
— Benjamin Franklin, *Poor Richard's Almanack* (1733)

Melons, too, have been cultivated since biblical times. There is an ancient Islamic saying that eating a melon produces a thousand good works, probably alluding to the many seeds contained in these edible members of the gourd family. The ancient Hebrews, according to Ebenezer Brewer, called certain stones on Mt. Carmel *Elijah's melons.* Allegedly the owner of the land refused to supply food for the prophet Elijah, and as punishment his melons were turned into stones.

Today the value of melons is still acknowledged in the informal use of *melon* to mean a windfall profit and the terms *to cut/split/slice the melon,* meaning to distribute bonuses or extra profits among investors, employees, or other participants in an enterprise.

As for Franklin's statement, the most experienced melon buyer will admit that it is extremely difficult to tell when a melon has ripened (or will ripen) to perfection.

Of the numerous varieties of melon, the largest is the *watermelon,* so called for its extremely juicy flesh. Its cultivation dates from prehistoric times, and it was brought to America with the first settlers and quickly adopted and cultivated by native Americans as well. During the nineteenth century it became extremely popular in rural areas, where a *watermelon patch* was found in most gardens. Perhaps because such large fruits (some weighing fifty pounds or more) could be shared by a large group, the melons were consumed on numerous social occasions known by such names as a *watermelon cutting, watermelon day,* or *watermelon party.* As late as 1948 a local Oklahoma newspaper, the *Daily Ardmoreite,* announced: "Stewards of the First Methodist Church have been invited to a water-melon cutting in Fellowship Hall of the Church Wednesday at 7:30 P.M."

Peachy-Keen

A *swell girl—you know—a regular peach.*
—George Ade, *Artie* (1896)

For more than two thousand years it was believed that peaches originated in Persia. The fruit's name comes from the Latin name for Persia, and peaches once were called *Persian apples.* However, modern botanists have found several kinds of peach native to China, and the fruit is mentioned in Chinese literature before 2000 B.C. Indeed, a 1938 book of *Racial Proverbs* by S. G. Champion quotes the Chinese proverb, "Rather one bite of a peach than eat a basketful of apricots," that is, rather a little of the best than a lot of the second best.

Given the widespread liking for this fruit, it is hardly surprising that the noun *peach* and related adjectives *(peachy, peachy-keen)* came to denote something or someone of superlative quality. The *OED*'s earliest citation for this usage is a letter by E. Turner written in 1754: "I had almost forgot that orange Peach, your niece." It continued to be so used well into the twentieth century.

Several terms alluding to the peach's appearance were transferred to an attractive complexion. The *peaches and cream complexion* (pink cheeks, creamy skin) promised by soap and face-cream manufacturers to those who used their products was first referred to around the turn of the twentieth century. However, Ralph Waldo Emerson had an earlier variant back in 1860 that may actually be the source of the later term: "It is the soundness of the bones that ultimates itself in the peach-bloom complexion" *(Conduct of Life: Beauty).* The *OED* cites his use of "peach-bloom" four years earlier still. In any event, it transfers the delicate powdery deposit on the skin of a ripe peach to the soft pink of the human complexion. (John Ciardi maintains that peaches and cream originally meant high living—peaches for delicious fruit, cream for the fat of the land—and that labor leaders of the turn of the century declared, "We'll all eat peaches and cream" when the labor movement was victorious, but he offers no verifying citations. This usage, if ever common, is now obsolete.) The skin of a peach is slightly fuzzy, and *peach fuzz* is informally used to describe the skin of an adolescent boy showing the faint beginnings of a beard.

"Peach" and "peachy" often but not always described women. F. Scott Fitzgerald wrote, "He's a peach of a fellow" in 1925, and James T. Farrell wrote, "He told himself that Airedales were peachy dogs" *(Studs Lonigan,* 1932). Although "peachy" for superlative is heard less often today, at least in America, a U. S. variant, *peachy-keen,* arose about 1955 and is still current, although often used ironically as in "Peachy-keen! I forgot to mail these letters."

The verb *to peach,* meaning to betray or inform on someone, has nothing to do with the fruit. It is a shortening of *impeach* that has been so used since the fifteenth century, although today it is considered mainly slang.

Pears

On the first day of Christmas
My true love gave to me
A partridge in a pear tree.
          —English carol, "The Twelve Days of Christmas"

Pears figure in a great many proverbs, from ancient sources to modern. "Plant pears for your heirs," alluding to the pear tree's slowness to yield, is recorded in a 1640 collection (Herbert, *Jacula Prudentum),* while Mao Tse-tung said, "If you want to know the taste of a pear, you must change the pear by eating it."

This ancient and popular tree fruit—the Roman writer Pliny named more than forty varieties—is known for its characteristic shape. In most varieties the fruit tapers toward the top and bulges toward the bottom, and it is this characteristic that is frequently transferred. Most women consider being called *pear-shaped* a less than flattering comment, but compared to men, many women's bodies do tend to be shaped in this way, a broader pelvis no doubt being an evolutionary adaptation to ease childbearing. Those who deplore the tendency may take comfort in the recent medical finding that this natural contour is associated with a lower risk of developing heart disease than that incurred by the slim-hipped.

Slightly less obvious is the term *pear-shaped tones,* which since the mid-eighteenth century has denoted a full-bodied vocal sound—clear, resonant, and without harshness. However, this also is occasionally used for a tone, played or sung, that bulges (swells or broadens) in the middle owing to imperfect control.

The name "pear" has also attached itself to other fruits, such as the *prickly pear,* a pear-shaped cactus that the poet T. S. Eliot substituted for the mulberry in "Here we go round the prickly pear at five o'clock in the morning" (*The Hollow Men*), and the *alligator pear,* another name for the pear-shaped, bumpy-skinned avocado.

Persimmons

This plumlike fruit, extremely sour when green but sweet when ripe, is no longer as common on American tables as it once was. The name itself is Algonquian and the fruit was known in earliest colonial times. Two slightly different varieties of the fruit grow in Asia.

In nineteenth-century frontier vernacular the persimmon surfaced in numerous phrases. A number of them involved comparison to the huckleberry (see under BERRIES above), but in others it stood alone. Thus, *to be a jump above his tallest persimmons* or *to pass his persimmon* both meant to be beyond his ken or understanding. *To bring down/walk off with the persimmon* meant to win the prize, and *the longest pole knocks the persimmon* meant that the best man wins. *To rake up/shake down the persimmons* meant to pocket the spoils. These terms all appear in nineteenth-century American sources from 1827 to about 1900 and clearly are obsolete. The *OED* lists one other, *That's [the ripe/all] persimmon,* for That's perfect/the best, as late as 1946, but it, too, is at best obsolescent.

Pineapples

He is the very pineapple of politeness.
  —Richard Brinsley Sheridan, *The Rivals,* 2:3 (1775)

This low tropical plant is a native of South America and is cultivated chiefly in the West Indies, Mexico, Florida, and Hawaii, the last having earned the name of *pineapple paradise* for its special suitability for growing the fruit. The name "pineapple" was also used for pine cones, which the fruit resembles.

The pineapple first was discovered by Europeans in the

mid-seventeenth century and was immediately prized for its sweet juiciness. It therefore came to be used as a synonym for "the pink of perfection," as seen in the quotation above. Dickens combined the two locutions, "The very pink and pineapple" (*Martin Chuzzlewit,* 1843), and it was still current nearly a century later, when Dudley Nichols wrote, "He is the soul of courtesy and the pineapple of perfection" (*New York World,* Nov. 24, 1926). By then its name had also been applied to a fragmentation hand grenade (*pineapple grenade),* a usage dating from World War I. Like the fruit, the surface of the grenade (also called *pineapple bomb*) had a crisscross pattern of lines marking the segments into which it would burst.

Plums and Prunes

He put in his thumb, and pulled out a plum,
And said what a good boy am I.
　　　　　　　—Nursery rhyme, "Little Jack Horner"

The plum tree, believed to be native to both the Eastern and Western hemispheres, grows wild in many temperate climates. Two principal varieties are cultivated, one for the fresh fruit and the other for making dried plums, or *prunes.*

In seventeenth-century England the word *plum* also signified a sum of one hundred thousand pounds, clearly a most desirable thing. Ebenezer Brewer records a "fanciful explanation" for the Jack Horner of nursery-rhyme fame, who pulled a plum out of a Christmas pudding. Allegedly Horner was steward to the Abbot of Glastonbury at the time when King Henry VIII abolished all monasteries. As required, the deeds to the abbot's twelve manor houses were sent to the king, hidden inside a pie, for safety. Jack Horner was the bearer, and en route he lifted a corner of the piecrust and pulled out the deed to the manor of Mells, which he kept and where he and his descendants lived for generations.

Since the early nineteenth century a *plum* has simply meant a good or desirable thing, such as an excellent position ("a plum of a job"), or a windfall profit ("the company's year-end bonus was a real plum").

> *The children were tucked all snug in their beds,*
> *And visions of sugarplums danced in their heads.*
> —Clement Clark Moore, "A Visit
> from St. Nicholas" (1823)

The *sugarplum* is not, as some might speculate, a sugar-coated fruit, but a small confection made of sugar and various other ingredients. Resembling the fruit in being roughly oval or round in shape, it has been so called since the early seventeenth century. However, a figurative use of the term dates from the same period, and it is not known which usage came first. Figuratively a sugarplum is anything pleasing or nice, especially when offered as a sop or a bribe. Thomas Dekker had it in *Langthorne and Candlelight* (1608): "By stopping the Constable's mouth with sugar-plummes (thats to say) whilst she poisons him with sweete wordes." More common in Britain than in America, this term may now be obsolete.

In Britain a *plum pudding* is a traditional Christmas dessert. This steamed or boiled confection usually contains raisins, currants, and other fruits, which may or may not include plums. When it does, they often are of the dried kind known as *prunes.* (See also PUDDING in the chapter on sweets.)

Pronouncing the word "prune" causes one to pucker up one's lips, a fact taken note of in the mid-nineteenth century in teaching ladies facial exercises and elocution. Charles Dickens spelled it out in *Little Dorrit* (1857): "Papa, potatoes, poultry, prunes and prism are all very good words for the lips; especially prunes and prisms." Apparently "prunes and prisms" was actually used by educators in this way, for it is referred to periodically until about 1900.

In America the wrinkled aspect of prunes has been transferred to a frowning face and disagreeable disposition, in such slang epithets as *prune face.* In Britain, particularly in armed forces slang, a *prune* is a stupid, hopelessly incompetent individual.

Rhubarb

Rhubarb is a low-growing perennial, a native of northeast Asia. It requires little care and now is cultivated the world over. The edible portion is the tender hollow stalk that holds up the large, thick leaves, which themselves are poisonous. It is extremely tart to the taste and therefore is almost exclusively served cooked with a quantity of sugar or another sweetener.

The principal transfer of *rhubarb* is to mean a heated argument or dispute. This usage was popularized by the famous baseball sportscaster Red Barber, who first used it in 1938 to describe a game-stopping melee. Barber said he got it from someone else, but he continued to use it, in broadcasts and in his 1968 book, *Rhubarb in the Catbird Seat.* Subsequently it was applied to a similar fracas anywhere, not just on a ball field. The precise allusion is unclear. Perhaps it comes from the fact that rhubarb is usually served stewed, and the word *stew* is used to mean a state of agitation. Or perhaps it is the appearance of cooked rhubarb, which resembles a tangle, much as a free-for-all does. Still another possible source is that in British theatrical productions, extras repeat the word "rhubarb" over and over to simulate a noisy crowd. However, none of these theories has been satisfactorily verified.

The rhubarbs, always in plural form, became a slang term for a rural area or small town around 1900 and is still occasionally heard.

THREE

Eat Your Vegetables!

Then a sentimental passion of a vegetable fashion
Must excite your languid spleen.
                                      —W. S. Gilbert, *Patience* (1880)

Vegetables, in the sense of food, are plants cultivated for some edible part, such as the tuber of a potato, the leaf of lettuce, or the flower buds of broccoli. They are nutritionally important, to the extent that they can be entirely relied on to sustain life and good health (and vegetarians do so; see below). Vegetables are very widely acknowledged to be good for you, but they are not universally loved. Hence the admonition *Eat your vegetables* has long and often been uttered in nurseries and at dinner tables.

Figuratively, a *vegetable* is a dullard, a person so impaired that his or her mental processes are nonexistent. This condition, of course, is the dreaded *vegetable state* of the comatose or brain-injured. However, the term "vegetable" is also used for individuals so passive and boring that they might as well be inanimate. Or, as Gilbert put it, poking further fun at the languid poses of the nineteenth-century aesthete, "If he's content with a vegetable love which would certainly not suit *me* / Why, what a most particularly pure young man this pure young man must be."

*If you become a vegetarian, you separate from your ancestors
and cut off posterity.*
                                   —G. Champion, *Racial Proverbs* (1938)

This Chinese proverb pokes the same sort of fun at *vegetarians,* individuals who avoid eating meat and other animal products for reasons ranging from ethics to health faddism. The most extreme of them regard eating meat as no better than cannibalism. However, the opposite view has also been expressed. "Most vigitaryans I iver see looked enough like their food to be classed as cannybals," observed Finley Peter Dunne *(Mr. Dooley's Philosophy,* 1900). The term *vegan* has been coined for those who avoid all animal products, not just meat but fish, eggs, dairy products, honey, and the like. *Ovolactarians,* on the other hand, will consume eggs and dairy products but no meat.

A couple of related terms have arisen in the closing decades of the twentieth century. One is *veggie,* which is simply short for "vegetable." Another is *to veg out,* American slang for entering a figurative vegetative and presumably restful and nonproductive state, as in, "We have no plans for Sunday; I'm just going to veg out."

Asparagus

Quicker than boiling asparagus.
                                   —Caesar Augustus, c. 27 B.C.

To those who have often eaten soggy, overcooked fresh asparagus or the limp canned variety, the simile here cited may seem puzzling. Yet it was quoted by Erasmus *(Adagia,* 1523) as a common figure of speech whenever anyone wanted something done speedily.

To those who are fond of it, the edible green shoots of this relative of the lily are a prized delicacy. As with all such tastes, and particularly with vegetables, love of asparagus is far from universal. Thus P. G. Wodehouse wrote, "Have you ever seen Spode eat asparagus? . . . Revolting. It alters one's whole conception of man as Nature's last word" *(The Code of the Woosters,* 1938).

Such comment notwithstanding, asparagus has been cultivated since ancient times. Moreover, the vegetable is the subject of one of John Ciardi's famous "spook etymologies," his label for invented word origins that have no basis in fact. He cites the derivation of "asparagus" from *sparrow grass,* accompanied by the explanation that sparrows are fond of the vegetable, much as catnip appeals to cats. This derivation is pure invention, for the name *asparagus* comes from the Greek *asparagos,* meaning a vegetable shoot. The medieval Latin word for it dropped the initial *a,* making it *sparagos,* and versions of this entered the English language, among them *sperage, sparagrass,* and *sparrow grass.* The last persisted as the polite name for the vegetable until about 1800, but had nothing whatever to do with birds.

During World War II an *asparagus bed* was military slang for an antitank device that resembled a bed of the vegetable, that is, lines of concrete set at an angle pointing toward the enemy and armed with explosives. This usage appears to have died out. Other terms involving asparagus are more obvious, such as the *asparagus beetle,* which feeds on the plant, and the *asparagus bean* and *asparagus fern,* plants that resemble the vegetable plant in some respects.

Avocado

This tree fruit is more often eaten as a vegetable, in the form of soups, salads, and sauces. Its name originally came from an Aztec word for the fruit, *ahuacatl,* which Spanish settlers confused with the word *abogado,* for lawyer. In English the fruit also is called *alligator pear,* for its pear shape and the fact that it allegedly grew in areas infested by alligators (a folk etymology).

Today the avocado's principal linguistic transfer is to the name of a color *(avocado,* or *avocado green),* a dull green resembling the flesh of the fruit. It enjoyed a period of extreme popularity among American interior decorators from the late 1940s to the 1960s. They in turn influenced the makers of household appliances such as refrigerators and washing machines, suppliers of bathtubs and sinks and the like, who offered this fashionable shade to customers.

Full of Beans

Beans appear in more idioms, proverbs, and slang than any other vegetable and have done so for many centuries. Beans variously denote the head (in *bean ball),* a vote *(devourer of beans, abstain from beans),* a small amount *(doesn't know beans),* money *(hasn't a bean),* good fortune *(find the bean in the cake),* information *(spill the beans),* and energy *(full of beans),* to mention just a few.

There are many kinds of bean, all of them the edible and highly nutritious seedpods and seeds of members of the legume family. (The name "bean" is also used for the seed of unrelated plants, such as the coffee bean or vanilla bean, but they are not under consideration here.) Green beans or snap beans are a familiar garden vegetable, as are wax beans or butter beans, similar in appearance but yellow in color. In both the pod is the part that is eaten.

More widespread and more nutritious, often functioning as a substitute for meat protein, are those varieties whose seed is the principal edible portion. Chief among these are the lima bean, navy or pea bean, kidney bean, and soy bean. The last is among the most useful of all seeds, being made into numerous products (both edible and nonedible). In linguistic transfers, too, it is the seed of bean plants that crops up most often. However, another bean-plant property, that of fast growth, is exploited in the fairy tale of *Jack and the Beanstalk,* in which Jack exchanges his impoverished mother's cow for a handful of beans that produce stalks reaching the sky. Jack climbs up them and is able to steal rich treasures from the evil giant's castle, so he and his mother are no longer poor.

> *When our recent Tutor is heard to speak,*
> *This truth one certainly gleans,*
> *Whatever he knows of Euclid and Greek,*
> *In Latin he doesn't know beans.*
> —*Yale Literary Magazine,* 1855

The very ubiquitousness of beans probably helped equate them with something of little worth, or, as in the usage above, with something of no worth. *Not to know beans* was American slang by the 1830s and persists to the present day. *Not worth a bean* is much older, appearing in Chaucer's *Troilus and Cressida* (c. 1380: "Switch arguments ne been nat worth a bene") and even earlier writings. From this it was but a small step to equate beans with money, as in *I haven't a bean,* meaning I haven't any money. The low worth of beans is also reflected in the word *beanery* for an inexpensive, third-rate restaurant, so used in America since the late nineteenth century.

A similar term, also American in origin, is not to amount to *a hill of beans,* first used in the mid-nineteenth century and still heard today (along with the variant *row of beans*). Both refer to planting practices. The first means placing the seeds in clumps (four or five to a clump) in a little mound of soil, or "hill"; the second alludes to the conventional commercial practice of long rows.

Another planting practice, that of staking the long vines, gave rise to the transfer of *beanpole* to mean a tall, slender individual.

Beanball

> *Tobacco is a dirty weed . . .*
> *It takes the hair right off your bean.*
> —G. L. Hemminger, 1915

The round shape of many beans probably is the source of the slang usage of *bean* for "head," which originated in the late nineteenth-century America. *To bean someone* means to hit someone on the head, a usage that probably came from baseball's *beanball,* a ball deliberately pitched at the batter's head in order to intimidate him. (It does not appear to be related to the earlier *I'll give him beans,* meaning I'll thrash him, which Brewer suggests may echo the French proverb, *S'il me donne des pois, je lui donnerai des fèves,* "If he gives me peas, I'll give him beans"—that is, tit for tat.)

The information inside someone's head, particularly secret information, has also been termed "the beans," mainly in the popular crime novel cliché, *spill the beans* (give away the secret). As for the outside of the head, in the United States a small, close-fitting hat or cap has been called a *beanie* since about 1940.

> *Abstain from beans.*
> —Pythagoras, *Maxims* (c. 525 B.C.)

Many old proverbs involve beans, and the precise meaning of some has been disputed. Take, for example, that of Pythagoras, quoted above and cited by Erasmus in his *Adagia* (1523). Aristotle held that it meant to abstain from venery, because the bean resembles the human testicle. Cicero claimed that it meant to avoid beans because they engender intestinal gas, a problem still encountered by many consumers. But the interpretation most generally accepted today is the one proposed by Plutarch (c. A.D. 95), that is, *abstain from beans* meant "Stay out of politics." The reason is that beans were used in ancient Greece in voting. To vote for someone, you cast a bean into his helmet. This interpretation was repeated by John Lyly (in *Euphues,* 1579) and became the source of the expression *devourer of beans* for someone who grew fat from feeding on beans, that is, an individual who took a bribe in exchange for his vote (bean = ballot). This usage appeared in Robert Bland's *Proverbs* (1814) but is now obsolete.

Another obsolete usage is *to know how many beans make five,* meaning to be no fool, to know what's what. Brewer suggests it is related to an old riddle, "How many blue beans make five white ones?" The answer is "Five, if peeled." Anyhow, the expression appears in Cervantes's *Don Quixote* (1605) and was still in an 1894 collection of *Folk-Phrases* by G. F. Northall, but is rarely if ever heard today.

To find the bean in the cake, meaning to win a prize or, by extension, to be lucky, comes from the ancient custom of hiding a bean among the raisins in the cake made for Twelfth Night (the Feast of Epiphany, which falls on January 6). The person who finds the bean becomes Bean-King, that is, "king" of the party. This custom is mentioned by Montaigne in his essays (1580) and remains current in some localities.

The expression *beans are in flower* used to be an excuse for an individual's silly behavior. It was based on the former belief that the perfume of bean flowers causes light-headedness. It, too, is obsolete, along with the belief.

Finally, *every bean has its black,* meaning that nobody is perfect or everyone has some fault, alludes to the black "eye" found in some beans. This Roman proverb also is seldom heard today.

Beantown

> And this is good old Boston,
> The home of the bean and the cod,
> Where the Lowells talk only to Cabots,
> And the Cabots talk only to God.
> —John Collins Bossidy,
> "On the Aristocracy of Harvard" (1910)

In New England *baked beans,* pea beans cooked for hours with molasses and salt pork, are a traditional dish dating back to colonial times. The Puritan housewife soaked her beans all of Friday night, baked them all day Saturday, and served them fresh for the Saturday night meal (the beginning of Sabbath). Boston, in effect the capital of New England, acquired the name *Beantown* early on, and it has stuck.

Of somewhat later provenance is the British *bean-fest,* the annual employees' dinner, which has been so called since about 1800. The precise source of the name has been forgotten. Beans probably were served, or the *bean-goose,* a variety of goose known and so called for its love of beans, may have been prominent in the menu. In any event, the term, also spelled *bean-feast,* was extended to similar annual outings or festive occasions.

> *Full o' beans and benevolence!*
> —Robert S. Surtees, *Handley Cross* (1843)

Why being replete with beans should denote being full of vim and vigor is somewhat puzzling, but this usage has been around for at least a hundred and fifty years. For a time in England the term was used somewhat differently—to mean being too haughty and full of oneself—but this meaning did not survive.

A *beanbag,* on the other hand, originally did contain beans. A small cloth bag filled with dried beans, it was used in various children's games during the nineteenth century (and presumably similar versions existed earlier). In the second half of the twentieth century manufacturers came up with the *beanbag chair,* a much larger version typically made of simulated leather and filled with bean-sized pellets, which molds itself readily to the occupant's body.

In Britain the occupant's friend might address him or her as *old bean,* a colloquial familiarity that became extremely common in the early twentieth century but is seldom heard on this side of the Atlantic.

Red as a Beet

> *The smallest boy, with the whitest face, the most beetrooty nose . . . ever seen.*
> —Charles Dickens, *All Year Round* (1859)

The beet is principally a root vegetable, although the leafy tops *(beet greens)* also are eaten and its close relative, *Swiss chard,* is valued entirely for its leaves. But the British generally call the vegetable *beetroot.*

Not all beets have red roots. A totally different species, the *sugar beet,* has a longer, thinner white root, which long supplied much of the sugar used throughout the world. Nevertheless, the only commonly used figure of speech involving beets is *red as a beet,* which generally is used in an unflattering sense: red with shame, embarrassment, effort, anger. Both it and *beet red* have been around for centuries.

Cabbage

Cabbage. A familiar kitchen-garden vegetable about as large and wise as a man's head.
—Ambrose Bierce, *The Devil's Dictionary* (1881–1906)

Cabbage belongs to a large plant family that also includes *bok choy, broccoli, brussels sprouts, cauliflower, celery cabbage (Chinese cabbage), collards, kale,* and *kohlrabi.* Probably originating in Asia Minor, it has been cultivated since ancient times.

Over the centuries cabbage has been credited with many medicinal properties, ranging from curing snake bite to growing hair on bald spots. The Roman writer Cato gave an elaborate recipe for consuming cabbage so as to prevent becoming drunk (in *De Agri Cultura,* c. 150 B.C.), as well as devoting many pages to its numerous other benefits. Possibly it was the gas-producing or laxative effect of the vegetable that led the ancients to use the word metaphorically in the proverb *Twice-served cabbage is death,* cabbage here meaning words or statements that are repeated over and over. It is often ascribed to

Juvenal, who had it in *Satires* (c. A.D. 120), but some say he was merely repeating an old Greek adage.

Cabbage is easily grown, relatively cheap, and therefore considered a humble food. These attributes no doubt are responsible for the modern Greek proverb, *Better cabbage with peace than sugar with grumbling* (quoted by Negris, *Modern Greek Proverbs,* 1831); in other words, better a modest meal consumed peacefully than a feast with arguments. They also account for the Canadian term *cabbagetown,* meaning the poor sections of a city, where the inhabitants live on cabbage and not much else. By extension it came to be used for any economically depressed area.

Since the mid-nineteenth century *cabbage patch* has meant a small, unimportant thing or place, and was sometimes extended to a small town. Alice Hegan Rice's book, *Mrs. Wiggs of the Cabbage Patch* (1901) popularized the term. She described the setting as not a real cabbage patch, but "a queer neighborhood where ramshackle cottages played hop-scotch over the railroad tracks."

In the early 1980s a series of soft-bodied *Cabbage Patch* dolls was marketed to American youngsters. Based on a design invented by artists in Appalachia, they were sold with a given name, birth certificate, and adoption papers, for their invention was based on the myth that new babies are found under cabbage leaves in a cabbage patch (a variation on the story that babies are brought by a stork). For a time they were sold by the millions, but as with all such fads their popularity has subsided.

The word "cabbage" is probably derived from *caput,* Latin for "head," alluding to the shape of the plant's tightly folded leaves. However, the term *cabbagehead* is not particularly flattering, having been used since the seventeenth century to signify a dolt. Neither is *cabbage pounder,* applied to an inept golfer who spends a good deal of time in the rough (shrubbery here being likened to cabbage leaves). On the other hand, *cabbage* is also an American slang term for money, especially paper money (which is green), and *my cabbage* is a colloquial term of endearment, thought to be a translation of the French equivalent, *mon chou.*

Finally, in American hospital jargon, *CABG,* pronounced "cabbage," is an acronym for *coronary arterial bypass graft,* a form of heart surgery being performed with increasing frequency.

Cabbage is not only eaten raw (in such salads as *cole slaw)* or cooked, but it also may be pickled. In this form it is generally known by its German name, *sauerkraut* (literally "sour cabbage"), and although it is a food known in many other countries, it is closely identified with Germany. Consequently the names *sauerkraut,* and later *kraut,* both became slang terms for Germans. The first was being used by the mid-nineteenth century in America; the second became popular on both sides of the Atlantic during World War I. Both usages are considered disparaging and offensive.

Training is everything ... cauliflower is nothing but cabbage with a college education.
—Mark Twain, *Pudd'nhead Wilson's Calendar* (1893)

Of cabbage's close relatives, only cauliflower has given rise to a linguistic transfer. Boxers sometimes develop *cauliflower ear,* a condition caused by repeated blows and the formation of scar tissue that makes the ear resemble the small florets of the cauliflower.

Carrot

The distinctively orange root of the carrot has been a popular vegetable for centuries. Carrots originally grew wild and came under cultivation only about two thousand years ago. Today there are some four hundred different commercial varieties.

Carrots are not an exclusively human food. Horses and donkeys love them, whence the figurative usage of *the carrot and the stick* to mean an enticement or reward and a punishment—that is, one dangled a carrot in front of a donkey to induce it to move forward and nudged it ahead by beating it with a stick from behind. The term has been so used since the late nineteenth century. During World War II British prime minister Winston Churchill used it in a speech about the Italian campaign: "We shall continue to operate on the Italian donkey at both ends, with a carrot and a stick" (May 25, 1943).

Other than that, the principal transfer of carrot has been an allusion to its bright orange color—in such slang terms as *carrot-top* or *carroty* for a redheaded individual, used since the seventeenth century (the latter mainly in Britain).

Corn

In America *corn* denotes a grain with edible seeds called kernels, which are used in a wide variety of ways. The variety of the plant that is used as a vegetable is called *sweet corn;* a related variety, *field corn,* is animal fodder but is also used to make oil and a number of other products. A native Western Hemisphere plant, corn is also known as *Indian corn* in America. In Britain, however, this plant and its seeds are called *maize,* whereas "corn" denotes the seed of any cereal plant, most often wheat in England but oats in Scotland, etc.

The word "corn" has been linguistically transferred in numerous ways, and in many instances it does not seem particularly important to differentiate between the British and American definitions. For example, Thomas Deloney wrote, "My folkes are so cornefed that we have much adoe to please them in their diet" (*Iack of Newbery,* 1597). In this context *cornfed* simply means well-fed, and it does not really matter whether the writer meant full of maize or of wheat. Another meaning of cornfed appears in Beaumont and Fletcher's 1619 play, *Monsieur Thomas* (4:6): "What, are you grown so corn-fed, goody Gillian, you will not know your father?" Cornfed here means "conceited" or "uppity," but this usage was short-lived.

A number of English proverbs involve corn. One of the earliest is "No corne without some chaffe," meaning nothing is perfect. Appearing in Randle Cotgrave's *Dictionary* of 1611, it clearly alludes to wheat rather than maize, which is never threshed. The same is true of "Corn and horn go together" (John Ray, *English Proverbs,* 1678), which is also put as *up corn, down horn.* In other words, when wheat (corn) is high, beef (horn) is cheap; the two products are always linked in this way. In the same collection Ray includes "You measure everyone's corn by your own bushel," meaning you tend to judge others by your own achievements, and here "corn" could refer to either grain.

The Corn Laws

Ye coops us up and tax our bread,
And wonder why we pine;
But ye are fat, and round, and red,
And filled with tax-bought wine.
— Ebenezer Elliott, *Corn-Law Rhymes* (1831)

The importance of the grain industry in England is evident in a long chapter of British history, the *Corn Laws*. This series of protectionist laws, in force from about 1360 to 1846, kept domestic prices up by levying heavy duties on imported grain. While these laws benefited landowners, they kept the prices of flour and bread artificially high and thus created considerable hardship for the poor. The effect was particularly devastating in Ireland, which could not raise enough grain of its own to meet domestic demand but could not afford to import grain at the high prices the duties created. Consequently Ireland became wholly dependent on its potato crop, and when a blight caused crop failures during the 1840s, more than a million persons starved to death and another two million emigrated. This catastrophe, along with a poor English harvest in 1845, finally enabled their opponents to repeal the hated Corn Laws.

Corn High

The corn is as high as an elephant's eye,
And it looks like it's climbing right up to the sky . . .
— Oscar Hammerstein II,
"Oh, What a Beautiful Mornin' " (1943)

Although America does not, of course, have any native elephants to measure against, its farmers pride themselves on the height of their corn stalks. "I was born in Chicago . . . and railroaded ever since I was corn high," wrote A. C. Gunter (*Miss Dividends,* 1893).

Like other grains, corn also is made into distilled spirits, and *corn whiskey* has been so called in America since about 1830. Even earlier *corned* was slang for intoxicated. The English writer Francis Grose had it in his *Dictionary of the Vulgar Tongue,* and an issue of the *Massachusetts Spy* (December 22, 1823) had the ditty:

> *"Pretty well corned" and "up to anything,"*
> *Drunk as a lord and happy as a king.*

This usage did not survive the nineteenth century, nor did another term, *to acknowledge the corn,* meaning to admit the truth of something. This last is thought to have been invented by A. Stewart in an 1828 congressional debate, where Congressman Wickliffe of Kentucky admitted that one of the states claiming to export corn actually only fed corn to its hogs and exported it in that form. Stewart said Wickliffe thus had acknowledged the corn. The term remained current in America for about half a century but is now obsolete.

Corny

> *I'm as corny as Kansas in August,*
> *High as a kite on the Fourth of July.*
> — Oscar Hammerstein II,
>   "I'm in Love with a Wonderful Guy" (1949)

Originally *corny* simply meant pertaining to corn, and it was so used in Britain from the sixteenth century on. It may still have that meaning in the song quoted above, from the musical *South Pacific,* since Kansas is one of America's chief corn producers. But it may also have a double meaning, for in twentieth-century slang it means trite and mawkishly sentimental, appealing to the unsophisticated. John Ciardi held that it originated about 1890 in American show business, when actors from New York deemed themselves superior to country yokels, whom they termed *cornfed,* shortened to "corny." However, while his derivation and country of origin are correct, Ciardi offered no verifying citations for this early date. The first documented appearances of the word date from the early 1930s, when it was used by jazz musicians. Today, of course, it has far more general applications.

> *Jimmie crack corn an' I don't care,*
> *Ol' Massa's gone away.*
> —Dan Emmett, "The Blue-Tail Fly" (1846)

Corn cracker was an early 1830s term for a country yokel and alluded to the frontier staple food, cracked corn (which also figures in the above-quoted refrain of a popular minstrel song). Similar names cropping up in subsequent decades, all meaning rustic, were *cornthrasher, corn husker,* and *corn yokel.*

The much newer *cornball* is used as both noun and adjective. The noun denotes not only a corny person or thing but a confection of popcorn and molasses or caramel that is rolled into a ball. *Popcorn,* incidentally, is a particular kind of corn that makes the familiar fluffy white snack when it is heated until the kernel bursts (with a loud pop). Patricia Linden once described it as "the sentimental good-time Charlie of American foods" (in *Town and Country,* May 1984). This name, an abbreviation for "popped corn," has been used since about 1810. It is occasionally transferred to objects that resemble it, such as rounded chips of Styrofoam packing material, or a type of knitting stitch.

Baseball players of the early 1900s coined the term *can of corn* for an easy fly ball. It alludes to the practice of storing cans of corn on a high grocery-store shelf. To serve a customer, the grocer tipped the can forward with a broom handle and caught it.

Among the newest transfers is *cornrow,* for an African-American hairstyle in which the hair is parted into numerous neat rows and each section is tightly braided flat to the scalp. The style is not new, but the word first appeared in print in 1971, both as a noun and a verb. The allusion, of course, is to the rows in which corn is planted, which in states like Kansas may stretch as far as the eye can see.

Cool as a Cucumber

Young maids were as cold as cucumbers.
—Beaumont and Fletcher, *Cupid's Revenge,* 1:1 (1615)

The fruit of the cucumber vine has been used as a vegetable—mostly raw—since ancient times. It is thought to have originated in India and has been cultivated since antiquity in western Asia. A Chinese ambassador discovered cucumbers in use in Persia (Iran) in 200 B.C. and took some home with him. In the 1600s an English sea captain returning from the West Indies brought back pickled gherkins to the wife of Samuel Pepys and thus inspired their cultivation in England. "A cucumber now is better than a pumpkin in the future" appears in the Babylonian Talmud (c. A.D. 450) and refers to the vegetable's rapid growth compared to its relative, the pumpkin.

The cool temperature of cucumbers was observed long ago, and consequently *cool as a cucumber* has long been used as a synonym for self-possession. A recent study found that the inside of a cucumber in the field on a warm day is actually twenty degrees cooler than the air temperature.

Not everyone values cucumbers. Boswell quoted Samuel Johnson as saying, "A cucumber should be well sliced, and dressed with pepper and vinegar, and then thrown out, as good for nothing" *(Tour to the Hebrides,* Oct. 5, 1773), and he was allegedly quoting a common saying of English physicians.

Much of the modern cucumber crop is devoted to making pickles, that is, cucumbers preserved in brine and/or vinegar. The word *pickle* itself is thought to come from Dutch or German words for brine, a medium of preservation used not only for cucumbers but other vegetables, meats, and fish. To be *in a pickle,* meaning to be in an unpleasant predicament, is a very old expression indeed. A version of it appears in Dante's *Divine Comedy* (in Italian), and it turns up in several late sixteenth-century English writings. *A rod in pickle,* on the other hand, means to be in readiness for punishment; this phrase has been so used since the sixteenth century but mainly in Britain.

To be pickled, literally meaning to be steeped in brine, has also meant to be intoxicated since the seventeenth century. Although pickled herring is a popular dish in the Netherlands, North Germany, and Scandinavia, the word *pickle-herring* also means a clown or buffoon, taken from the name of a humorous character in a seventeenth-century German play. It was popularized by English journalist Joseph Addison in *The Spectator* in 1711 and consequently adopted into English.

Garlic

He could eat my heart with garlic. That is, he hates me mortally.

—John Ray, *English Proverbs* (1670)

Garlic is without question the strongest-tasting and strongest-smelling member of the onion family. Its bulb is divided into small "cloves," and it is used principally as a seasoning. In some parts of the world, however, it serves virtually as a vegetable, as, for example, the main ingredient of garlic soup.

Used since ancient times, garlic today is particularly associated with the cuisine of Mediterranean countries. Hence when north Europeans sometimes speak with contempt of southerners, a *garlicky* smell is one of the characteristics they complain about. In this spirit, *Garlic Wall* became the somewhat offensive name applied by Gibraltar's residents to a Spanish frontier barrier set up in 1969, when Spain was claiming ownership of Gibraltar. (The territory had belonged to Great Britain since 1713; in 1985 Spain conceded and reopened the frontier.)

The smell of garlic is, of course, its outstanding feature. "Garlicke makes a man winke, drinke, and stinke," Thomas Nashe observed in 1594 *(Unfortunate Traveller),* a rhyme that was repeated numerous times over the years. Medicinal values also were (and are) ascribed to it. Before the era of antibiotics, garlic was widely used to control infection. It also has been used against asthma, hypertension, and numerous other disorders. Further, doctors refer to a swelling of the last joint of the finger, caused by arthritis, as *garlic finger* (for its resemblance to the bulb).

The ancients believed that garlic could destroy the magnetic power of the lodestone, a theory subscribed to by Pliny and Plutarch, among others, but by about 1650 this belief had been exposed as erroneous (Sir Thomas Browne discussed it in his *Vulgar Errors*).

Leeks

This mild-tasting member of the onion family is the national emblem of Wales. Legend has it that St. David caused his countrymen under King Cadwaladr to distinguish themselves from the Saxon enemy by wearing a leek in their caps. According to Shakespeare, the Welsh wore leeks at the Battle of Poitiers ("the Welshmen . . . wearing leeks in their Monmouth caps; which . . . is an honourable padge of the service," *Henry V*, 4:7). In the same play Shakespeare uses the leek in another figure of speech. "He is come to me and bid me eat the leek," meaning he is making me eat my words.

We may say that an apple a day keeps the doctor away, but in the sixteenth century the leek was credited with the same salubrious qualities. "Leekes purgeth the bloud in march," wrote William Bullein (*Government of Health*, 1558), and a century or so later John Aubrey advocated this spring tonic more poetically (*The Natural History of Wiltshire*, c. 1685):

Eat Leekes in Lide [*March*] *and*
    Ramsins [*wild garlic*] *in May,*
And all the year after Physitians may
    play.

Lettuce

Lettuce is like conversation: it must be fresh and crisp, so sparkling that you can scarcely notice the bitter in it.
—Charles Dudley Warner,
My Summer in the Garden (1871)

Lettuce is the main member of the group called *salad greens,* which also includes escarole, endive, sorrel, watercress, and arugula, among others. In all of them it is the leaf that is eaten, most often raw.

Lettuce, too, has been known for centuries. It figures in the Roman proverb *Like lips, like lettuce,* meaning like attracts like; it alludes to the donkey eating a thistle as human lips might eat lettuce.

In modern times, *lettuce* is slang for paper money, a usage that probably began as underworld argot around 1900 and later became more widespread. (Also see SALAD DAYS.)

Mushrooms

The mushroom is a fungus, belonging to an entirely different group of plants from the common vegetables. Many kinds of wild mushroom grow in dark, damp places, in forests and beneath logs and stones, but some grow well in open pasture. Some wild mushrooms are edible, but others are lethally poisonous.

The features of mushrooms that have most often occasioned linguistic transfers are their habit of rapid growth and shape. John Florio was not even exaggerating when he wrote, "In one night growes a Mushrop" (*First Fruites,* 1578). Consequently, in colloquial use a *mushroom* denotes anything that springs up overnight or at any rate very quickly—a person, an institution, a city. Similarly, the verb *to mushroom* has meant to grow very quickly since about 1900.

As for shape, in Britain *mushroom* is slang for an umbrella, which it does indeed resemble. In late nineteenth-century American slang, according to sociologist Irving Lewis Allen, *mushroom fakers* were street vendors of umbrellas, and this term, shortened to *mush faker,* then was extended to mean an itinerant peddler, tinker, or umbrella mender.

The most dramatic transfer, however, occurred with the first testing of nuclear devices in the 1940s. William L. Laurence reported his view of an atom bomb test in the *New York Times:* "At first it was a giant column that soon took the shape of a supramundane mushroom" (Sept. 26, 1945). He was not the only one drawing this analogy, and ever since *mushroom cloud* has described the cloud of dust and particles resulting from a nuclear explosion.

Onions

Onions can make ev'n heirs and widows weep.
—Benjamin Franklin, *Poor Richard's Almanack* (1734)

The onion is one of the few modern plants mentioned in the Bible. In the Book of Numbers it is recorded that the Israelites complained to Moses as they were being led out of Egypt, "We remember the fish which we did eat in Egypt freely; the cucumbers and the melons, and the leeks and the onions and the garlick." The workers who built the Great Pyramid are recorded to have consumed onions, radishes, and garlic costing 1,600 talents (said to be equal to $2 million).

The onion family includes a number of similar plants, notably shallots, scallions or green onions, and chives (see also LEEKS; GARLIC). Of these, it is the onion that contains an oil whose pungent odor makes the eyes tear. Franklin was far from the first to make this observation (quoted above). It was mentioned as long ago as 610 B.C. It also led to the British expression *to take out (the) onion,* meaning to fake deep emotion.

The onion is a rounded bulb consisting of close concentric layers. It has no real center. Consequently some writers have used it as a simile for something that has no core. In his play *Peer Gynt* (1867), exposing the hero's heartlessness, Henrik Ibsen wrote: "You're not an emperor, you're an onion! Now, my dear Peer, I'm going to peel you, however little you may enjoy it" (5:5). Similarly, the American critic James Gibbons Huneker wrote, "Life is like an onion; you peel off layer after layer and then you find there is nothing in it."

Despite its lack of a center, the onion appears in the saying *to know one's onions,* meaning to know one's subject well, or to be extremely proficient. It dates from about 1920 but is heard less often today.

Several other attributes of onions have been transferred. Their outermost layer is quite thin, leading to the name *onionskin* for very thin, virtually transparent paper. For a time in late nineteenth-century America it had a still more specific meaning, that is, for "tissue ballots"—ballots on such thin paper that a large number could be stuffed into a ballot box. By extension, therefore, *onionskin ballots* became synonymous with the stuffing of ballot boxes. However, this usage, mentioned in the Congressional Record of 1879, appears to have been short-lived, and by the 1890s onionskin simply meant a fine grade of thin, translucent paper used for typewriting and similar purposes.

The bulbous shape of onions led to the term *onion dome* in church architecture. It refers to a bulblike roof ending in a sharp point or spire. Although this term first appeared in print only in the 1950s and then was applied to Russian Orthodox churches, the shape is much older and is widespread in other places, as, for example, in the Roman Catholic churches of Bavaria.

Parsley

Parsley is gharsley.
—Ogden Nash, "Further Reflections on Parsley" (1942)

In practice, few individuals actually object to parsley, another of the so-called salad greens. Of Mediterranean origin, its leaves are used to flavor food. Attractive in appearance, it often is used as a garnish. The ancient Greeks decked tombs with parsley because it stays green for a long time. This practice gave rise to the expression "He has need now of nothing but a little parsley," meaning he is dead.

Another saying popular from the seventeenth to nineteenth centuries was, "The child comes out of the parsley bed," which alluded to the belief that parsley has aphrodisiac properties. This idea has never been verified, but modern herbalists have discovered that parsley is an effective diuretic.

Like as Two Peas

As lyke as one pease is to an other.
—John Lyly, *Euphues* (1580)

Pea is the name given to several thousand species belonging to the legume family, which also includes beans, alfalfa, clover, and many other plants whose seeds are contained in pods. Pea pods, which grow on climbing vines, split easily in two and contain two to ten round, sweet seeds. Some varieties of pea are grown solely for their seeds, others for both pods and seeds, and still others, such as the sweet pea, for their flowers. They also are raised for fodder.

Peas were used by the Chinese as early as 2000 B.C. and are mentioned in the Bible. In England, however, they came to be looked on as a low form of food. That view is reflected in the reply attributed to Beau Brummel when asked if he ever ate vegetables: "I once ate a pea" (c. 1800).

The individual seeds contained in a pea pod are indeed very much alike, whence the old simile *as like as two peas in a pod.* Other attributes that have been transferred are similarly obvious. A *peashooter,* which is a toy weapon, is a tube through which dried peas or beans or pellets resembling them are blown; the term dates from the mid-nineteenth century. *Pea coal* alludes to very small pieces of coal, not much larger than actual peas. *Pea green* is a shade of medium, yellowish green. A *pea-soup fog* is a very thick fog, soup made from dried peas (split peas) generally being quite thick.

One nineteenth-century American term, *the last of pea-time,* may need more explanation. *Pea-time* simply meant the season when peas ripen. By extension the end of this season came to mean the end of anything, and the attendant sadness of an ending. However, the expression appears to have virtually died out.

An earlier spelling of peas, *pease,* survives in the nursery rhyme, "*Pease-porridge* hot, pease-porridge cold, pease-porridge in the pot, nine days old." It refers to a British dish, a kind of pudding made with dried peas.

One-Potato, Two-Potato ...

Pray for peace and grace and spiritual food,
For wisdom and guidance, for all these are good,
But don't forget the potatoes.
—John Tyler Pettee (1822–1907), "Prayer and Potatoes"

The Irish or white potato is one of the most important human foods. Native to the Americas, it was first cultivated in South America and was brought to Europe by Spanish explorers about 1550. It is now grown in every cool climate of the world, although it cannot tolerate much frost.

Given its relatively recent arrival in English-speaking countries, a remarkable number of terms involve the potato, which is probably a testament to the importance of this widespread tuber. Among the oldest still current is *small potatoes,* meaning something unimportant. The English poet Samuel Taylor Coleridge first had it as *little potatoes* (in a letter of 1797), but in America it became the more usual "small," which persists. Davy Crockett wrote, "This is what I call small potatoes, and few of a hill" (1836).

In Britain *clean potatoes* has meant, since about 1820, something excellent, proper, and/or reliable. In Australia *potato* is short for *potato peeler,* which is rhyming slang for Sheila, in turn slang for a girl or woman. None of these is heard much in America. However, another term of British provenance, *to drop like a hot potato,* meaning to drop something very fast, dates from about 1840 and remains current in Britain and America. (Because the tuber contains considerable water, it retains heat, so it is easy to burn one's fingers on it.) By extension, a *hot potato* has come to mean an issue or circumstance that is too difficult to handle. And in medicine, doctors refer to a patient with inflammation of the epiglottis as having *hot-potato voice.*

*Only two things in this world are too serious
to be jested on—potatoes and matrimony.*

—Irish saying

Potatoes have played a role in history as well. Probably the most famous instance is the notorious Irish *potato famine* of the 1840s, which caused widespread starvation and subsequent emigration (see CORN LAWS). A century later, a merchant sea captain, D. J. Jones, earned the nickname *Potato Jones* when he tried to run General Franco's blockade off Spain in 1937 with a steamer loaded with potatoes.

Potatoes are always eaten cooked but are served in numerous forms—boiled, baked, mashed, fried, fried and dried (potato chips, sticks, crisps, etc.), in salad, etc. The name of at least one form, *mashed potatoes,* has been transferred by skiers to heavy, wet snow that resembles that dish.

Potatoes figure in a number of children's games as well. Probably the best known of them is the *potato race,* dating from the 1880s. In it each player must carry a number of potatoes, one at a time and usually in a spoon, from one place to another (the first to finish successfully wins). Another is *hot potato,* a version of musical chairs in which all but one of the players is given a potato to hold. When the music starts, they must pass the potatoes to their left as quickly as possible; when the music stops the player who has no potato is eliminated. Finally, *one-potato, two-potato* is a playground method of choosing the player who will be "It" in tag, hide-and-seek, or some other game. The participants put out their hands, formed into fists (resembling potatoes?), and one of them touches each fist in turn, saying, "One-potato, two-potato, three-potato, four, five-potato, six-potato, seven-potato more, y-o-u are It!" ("It" being the one on whose fist the verse ends).

The most recent addition to potato terminology is the *couch potato,* a term coined by Tom Iacino and friends for a group appearing in the Doo-Dah Parade of Pasadena, California, in 1979 and denoting a person who spends a great deal of time watching television, presumably as inert as a potato on the sofa. Some have suggested that it is derived from *boob tuber,* "boob tube" being slang for a television set, but its inventors have not verified this origin. Nevertheless, the term caught on very quickly in America, beating out such potential rivals as "sofa spud."

Sweet Potato

Let the sky rain potatoes.
—William Shakespeare, *The Merry Wives of Windsor,* 5:5

Despite its name the sweet potato is not at all related to the white potato. Although it is also a tuber, it belongs to the morning glory family. It, too, is a native of the Americas and was brought to Europe by early explorers. Further, it was supposed to have aphrodisiac qualities, which is what Falstaff is invoking in the quotation above. *Sweet potato* is also an informal name for the ocarina, a musical instrument that resembles it. It is actually a globe-shaped flute, made of pottery or plastic and having a mouthpiece and finger holes.

Some Pumpkins

You're some punkins at a hundred yards dash.
—Jack London, *Valley of the Moon* (1913)

The pumpkin, a member of the squash family, is more often used for a pie filling and in similar concoctions than as a vegetable. The pumpkin figures in the fairy tale of Cinderella (the coach returning her from the ball reverts to a pumpkin at midnight), and Ebenezer Brewer believed this led to the use of *pumpkin time* as signifying the end of prosperity and happiness, in effect a return to the normal state of affairs. Pumpkins also figure in a well-known nursery rhyme, but here their significance is more elusive:

> *Peter, Peter, pumpkin eater,*
> *Had a wife and couldn't keep her.*
> *He put her in a pumpkin shell,*
> *And there he kept her very well.*

The pumpkin, also spelled *punkin,* turns up in several New World locutions as well. The name *pumpkin head* was at one time applied to all New Englanders, because the Puritan Blue Laws prescribed that men wear their hair cut short all the way around their heads. The normal way to accomplish this was to place a cap over a man's head and cut all the hair protruding beyond its edge; allegedly when no cap was available, half a pumpkin shell was substituted. The name was not a flattering one, however, and soon acquired the connotation of doltishness and stupidity.

Exactly why *some pumpkins/punkins* should mean a person or matter of some importance and excellence is not known, but it appeared in America in the 1840s and is still occasionally heard.

Radish

Did but the radish digest its own self!
—J. L. Burckhardt, *Arabic Proverbs* (1817)

This pungent root, eaten mostly raw as a relish or in salads, grows wild and also has been cultivated for centuries. There is an ancient belief that radishes aid in the digestion of other foods but are themselves not digested. The proverb quoted above transfers this property to human affairs, that is, would that we could get rid of someone who has helped us.

A very common variety of radish is red on the outside and white within. This characteristic gave rise to *radish communist* for an individual who professes communist beliefs but is not really committed to them. This primarily British usage dates from about 1920 and also crossed the Atlantic, but is only occasionally heard today. A. M. Rosenthal, in a *New York Times* column reminiscing about his student days at City College of New York, wrote, "There was a handful of Communists on campus and a few radishes—red outside, white inside. The rest of us focused on work. . . ." (April 20, 1993).

A close relative of the radish is the *horseradish,* so called not because horses love it but because the prefix "horse" for plants tends to denote a larger or coarser variety. The root of this plant is much more pungent than the radish's and is used principally as a condiment as well as in medicine. Herbalists claim it is a potent stimulant, and it has been used to clear nasal passages, reduce edema, as a digestive aid, and to fight infection.

Its pungent character has occasionally been transferred, as in John Galt's *Lawrie Rodd* (1849): "With a plentiful garnish of the horse radish of their petulance" (cited by the *OED).*

Salad Days

My salad days, when I was green in judgment.
—William Shakespeare, *Antony and Cleopatra*, 1:5

Although salad can denote a mixture of various foods—meat, fish, raw or cooked vegetables, eggs, fruits—served cold, the first thing that comes to mind with the word is LETTUCE or some other kind of *salad green*. And one of the oldest transfers of this word is the one invented by Shakespeare, *salad days*, meaning a time of youthful inexperience.

Another characteristic of salads, the fact that they often contain small amounts of a variety of foods, was transferred even earlier. "He that laboreth nothyng holy, but catcheth a patche of euery thing, is mete to pycke a salet," wrote Robert Whitinton (*Vulgaria*, 1520), who thus equated picking a salad with being engaged in trivia rather than important matters. Shakespeare, however, used similar wording with a slightly different meaning: " 'Twas a good lady: we may pick a thousand salads ere we light on such another herb" (*All's Well that Ends Well*, 4:5).

Today's *salad bar*, found in numerous American restaurants, allows customers to create their own salads, choosing from and combining a large variety of ingredients. And the word *salad* itself has been transferred to any variegated mixture since Shakespeare's time, as in "The team consisted of a salad of players, from Puerto Rico, the Dominican Republic, Mexico, and Brazil, as well as Florida."

The main ingredients of a salad are usually mixed with some kind of dressing, often based on oil and vinegar or on mayonnaise. "In a good salad there should be more oil than vinegar or salt," said St. Francis de Sales (c. 1600). Apart from being a recipe, this dictum can readily be interpreted to mean that an undertaking benefits more from smoothness and lubrication than from astringent or spicy qualities.

Spinach

"It's broccoli, dear."
"I say it's spinach, and I say the hell with it."
—E. B. White, *The New Yorker*, Dec. 8, 1928

Spinach was long used in Europe as a special dish for feast days. Nevertheless, it is not universally loved, as underlined by George Ade's quip, "One man's poison ivy is another man's spinach" (*Hand-Made Fables*, 1920).

In the United States the nutritious values of spinach were touted by Max Fleischer's famous film cartoon character, Popeye, created about 1933. When this tough sailor had to defend his girlfriend, Olive Oyl, against the evil Bluto, he fortified himself by eating spinach. This strategy was based on the idea that spinach contains considerable iron and the identification of iron with strength. Although spinach is rich in iron, most of it cannot be absorbed by the body, and further, iron is not precisely a factor in physical strength. Nevertheless, Popeye and spinach did catch on, to the extent that American mothers would exhort their children to eat spinach and become strong like Popeye.

However, E. B. White's caption to Carl Rose's cartoon of a mother and child at the dinner table, quoted above, uses *spinach* in the meaning of nonsense or rubbish. This American colloquialism was around from the 1920s to the 1950s but was not very common and is probably obsolete.

Tomatoes

It is hard to believe that tomatoes, which seem so essential to the cuisine of Italy, Spain, Greece, and other European countries, were unknown in Europe until introduced there by explorers who found them in the Western Hemisphere. However, only after they won wide acceptance in Europe were they used on a large scale in the United States. Until the early nineteenth century Americans believed them to be poisonous, owing to the fact that they belong to the nightshade family, which includes numerous poisonous species. From the French name for them, *pomme d'amour* or "love apple," came the practice of English youths presenting them to their sweethearts as a token of affection. Sir Walter Raleigh is said to have presented one to Queen Elizabeth I.

In twentieth-century American slang, a *tomato* is a girl or woman, a locution now considered offensive. Damon Runyon acknowledged that it was disrespectful in 1929, along with such terms as "doll" and "broad."

Turnips and Parsnips

There's no getting blood out of a turnip.
—Frederick Marryat, *Japhet in Search of a Father* (1836)

The root vegetable turnip is no longer as popular in America as in former times, when, in the absence of refrigeration, it was valued for its long keeping qualities. However, it has been a mainstay of north European diets for centuries. According to *New York Times* food writer Molly O'Neill, an anonymous writer of the fifteenth century compared the Dutch turnip eater to a swine digging for roots, and the sixteenth-century satirist Rabelais called the people of France's Limousin region "turnip chewers." The turnip is regarded somewhat contemptuously as the food of the poor, a fact reflected in the modern French slang use of *navet,* or "turnip," for an inferior painting.

In English a surprising number of old sayings involve turnips. The fact that the plant's root is eaten is transferred by numerous writers, such as Samuel Butler: "A degenerate nobleman, or one that is proud of his birth, is like a turnip. There is nothing good of him but what is underground" (*Characters,* c. 1660).

In nineteenth- and early twentieth-century slang *turnip* was humorously applied to a person, a mild way of calling him or her a dolt or knucklehead. It also was British slang for a large, old-fashioned silver watch, the kind dangled from a watch chain. This usage may be obsolete.

Turnips probably originated in Eurasia and may have been cultivated for as long as four thousand years. Prior to that they abounded in the wild. As pointed out, they are not considered a noble vegetable. They are easy to grow, and hence cheap and plentiful. It was probably these qualities Dickens was alluding to when he wrote, "It was as true . . . as turnips is. It was as true . . . as taxes is. And nothing's truer than them" (*David Copperfield,* 1850).

Another root vegetable whose popularity has diminished, at least in America, is the *parsnip,* but one old saying about it has survived from the seventeenth century to the twentieth. John Clarke had it in *Paroemilogia* (1639): "Fair words butter noe parsnips," meaning fine talk won't feed the family. It was still being said in the 1940s.

In Britain a number of slang expressions alluded to parsnips. *To look parsnips* means to look displeased or sour; *before you can say parsnips* means very quickly; *I beg your parsnips* is a joking version of "I beg your pardon." None of these crossed the Atlantic, and they may be obsolete in Britain as well.

FOUR

Beautiful Soup

Beautiful Soup, so rich and green,
Waiting in a hot tureen!
Who for such dainties would not stoop?
Soup of the evening, beautiful Soup!
　　　　—Lewis Carroll, *Alice in Wonderland* (1865)

Soup, whether thick as a *pea-soup fog* (see under PEAS) or a thin, flavorful broth, has been part of the human diet ever since the first cook combined meat or fish with water and boiled them. It was not always served as a first course, however. The ancient Romans usually began a formal meal with eggs in some form. By the sixteenth century or so, soup was the traditional beginning of such a meal, which would end with cheese. John Heywood's 1546 proverb collection had "In poste pace we past from potage to cheese"—that is, posthaste we passed from beginning to end, *potage* or *pottage* being the old word for a thick soup (*potage* still means "soup" in modern French). Today we are more apt to say *from soup to nuts* in the meaning of complete or all-inclusive, from beginning to end.

A nineteenth-century American expression that similarly alludes to a formal dinner is *soup-and-fish,* slang for the acme of male formal attire, white tie and tails. The most formal elaborate dinner includes both a soup course and a fish course.

Pottage also appears in some early versions of the warning,

Save your breath to cool your pottage, although "broth" and "porridge" appear in other versions. Whichever it is, they all mean the same thing: Don't bother voicing your thoughts on this issue.

Too Many Cooks . . .

Broth alone appears in several old sayings. Among the oldest is *Too many cooks spoil the broth,* first cited in 1580 and still current with the same meaning, that is, too many people working on a project will ruin it. A still older one, dating from 1545, is *As well to eat the devil as drink his broth*—a small sin is as bad as a big one—survived into the eighteenth century but is no longer heard today, when the devil and sin play a much smaller role in our lives and vocabulary.

Despite Mock Turtle's song quoted above, soup is present in a number of less positive expressions. To be *in the soup* has meant, since the late nineteenth century, to be in deep trouble;

the term presumably alludes either to falling into a kettle of soup, or, John Ciardi suggests, being chopped up and boiled. And patronizing a *soup kitchen,* a place where soup (and other food) is served to the needy, is hardly a wonderful experience. This term dates from the mid-nineteenth century; it first appeared in print in 1851. Unfortunately, it has seen a wide revival in the late twentieth century as a charitable enterprise for the homeless and urban poor. Finally, *soupy,* meaning thick or dense, has been extended to mean oversentimental or mawkish, as in, "This film is full of soupy deathbed scenes."

A somewhat more positive twentieth-century usage is *souped up,* a term originating in American racing slang to describe a supercharged motor engine. It later was extended to mean the charging up of other events, as in, "Announcing the guest of honor's surprise appointment really souped up the party."

Soup and broth are often made by boiling inexpensive bones and scraps, rather than large pieces of meat—so-called *soup bones.* In the early twentieth century the word *soup bone* became a slang term for a baseball pitcher's throwing arm, but it is not heard often nowadays.

The names of several particular soups have been transferred from time to time. We already mentioned the thickness of pea soup being applied to a thick fog. Another is *alphabet soup,* literally a broth containing pasta in the shape of letters of the alphabet. In the 1930s, when President Franklin Roosevelt's New Deal administration created many new government agencies often referred to by their initials (WPA, CCC, etc.), New York's former governor Al Smith quipped that the government was drowning "in a bowl of alphabet soup." Still another is *gumbo,* which F. Cuming described in 1810 as "made by boiling ocroe [okra] till it is tender and seasoning it with a little bit of fat bacon." Gumbo, which meant both okra and the soup, is an American dish native to Louisiana. It is thick and gelatinous in texture, so its name was transferred to a clay soil that becomes very sticky when it is wet. Further, in the late nineteenth century *gumbo* also referred to a black patois spoken in southern Louisiana.

Serving *chicken soup* on the eve of the Sabbath (Friday night) is a tradition in many Jewish households. So is a belief in this soup's curative qualities, whence the quasi-humorous term "Jewish penicillin" for chicken soup. Incidentally, this belief may not be unfounded; researchers in the 1990s found that chicken soup actually did ease the congestion and other symptoms of sufferers of the common cold more than other hot liquids.

Borscht and Chowder

Another soup favored by East European and Russian Jews is *borscht,* a concoction of beets and, sometimes, other vegetables, which is served both hot and cold. In the late 1930s it gave rise to the name *borscht circuit* (or *borscht belt*) for the hotels of a resort area in New York's Catskill Mountains that catered to a predominantly Jewish clientele, where borscht was often served and the guests were entertained by Jewish comedians.

A much older American soup is *chowder,* a thick soup containing fish or seafood (especially clams) along with vegetables (especially potatoes). Its name comes from the French (and French-Canadian) name for stew pot, *chaudière,* and it is particularly popular in New England. Possibly from it comes the expression *chowderhead* for a thick-skulled, dim-witted person, but there is some disagreement concerning the word's origin. John S. Farmer suggested that it may come from Anglo-Chinese slang, where *chowdar* means "fool" (in his *Americanisms,* 1889). Several other transfers of chowder are less problematic. In the mid-nineteenth century it was used in the sense of a heavy mixture, as in, "All is fish that comes to his net, and goes to make up the grand chowder of his political reputation" *(Arcturus,* December 1840).

John Ciardi held that *Chowder and Marching Society/Club* became an arch name for any festive social gathering. It alludes to the nineteenth-century American practice of holding politically sponsored outings, in which the participants marched through town to the site of their picnic, which featured chowder and beer.

Finally, we have *like duck soup,* which has been a simile for extremely easy since about 1910. Why duck soup should be characterized in this way is no longer known, but this Americanism became widely known when the Marx Brothers used it as the title of one of their funniest motion pictures, *Duck Soup* (1933).

FIVE

Cereal and Pasta

Cooked cereal today is widely regarded as breakfast food and as nursery food (it is one of the first solids fed to still toothless infants). Numerous grains—corn, wheat, oats, buckwheat—are turned into such foods simply by being ground and cooked with a quantity of water, which they absorb in the process. In America, cornmeal mush or grits were long used as a staple starchy food before they graced the breakfast table. Oatmeal was known in Britain from the time of the Roman invasion.

Wholesome Porridge

The halesome parritch, chief of Scotia's food.
        —Robert Burns, *The Cotter's Saturday Night*

Porridge, a cooked cereal most often made of oatmeal, has been a staple of the British diet for centuries. The old English word for it sometimes was *pottage,* leading to some confusion as to whether oatmeal or soup was meant in certain sayings. "Save your breath to cool your broth" also appeared as "pottage" and "porridge," all with the same meaning. A similar allusion is found in *"Blow thy own pottage, and not mine,"* meaning mind your own business. Neither of these is heard much today, at least not in America.

Another old proverb is *Old porridge is sooner heated than new made,* appearing in John Ray's 1670 collection and presumably meaning, make do with the old. His 1678 collection also had, *If it should rain porridge he would want his dish,* a dictum appearing in numerous other compendia and clearly meaning, be prepared so you can take advantage of opportunities when they arise. That adage crossed the Atlantic as well; "When it rains porridge, hold up your dish," wrote Sarah Orne Jewett in 1895 *(Life of Nancy).*

More puzzling is one saying that appears in numerous early collections but has died out: *I know him not though I should meet him in my porridge.* Presumably it means I wouldn't recognize this person even though he might appear in the most familiar setting imaginable.

The *Oxford English Dictionary* provides several other locutions involving porridge. Figuratively, *porridge* is a conglomeration of various things, a hodgepodge, and *to make a porridge* means to make a mess of something. Ebenezer Brewer's Dictionary included a few more sayings: *everything tastes of porridge,* meaning whatever we may imagine or pretend, the homely and familiar will prevail; *he has supped all his porridge,* meaning he's eaten his last meal (is dead); *not to earn salt for one's porridge,* not to earn enough to make a living, and by extension, to be too lazy to do so; and *to do porridge,* to serve time in jail. This last dates from the mid-twentieth century and gained currency in the 1970s through a popular British television show, *Porridge,* a situation comedy about life in prison.

All of the foregoing terms are better known in Britain than in America, where *oatmeal* is the more widely used term. It has given its name to a shade of grayish tan that resembles the cereal's color.

Oats is the principal grain of Scotland, as Burns points out in the poem quoted above. "All the world is otemeale, and my poke is left at home" is Brian Melbancke's rueful version of the "raining porridge" caution, Be prepared (in *Philotimus*, 1583). In Scottish universities, *Oatmeal Monday* is the name given to the midterm Monday, when the fathers of poorer students brought them a sack of oatmeal to feed them for the remainder of the term.

Pasta

Although *pasta* is the Italian word for "paste," with luck any resemblance should end right there. Since the second half of the nineteenth century this name has been used in English for the large variety of foods made from coarsely ground durum wheat that is kneaded with water and/or eggs to make the many shapes of macaroni and noodles.

> *Yankee Doodle came to town,*
> *Riding on a pony,*
> *Stuck a feather in his cap*
> *And called it macaroni.*
>
> —Edward Bangs (c. 1775)

At the time this ditty was written, *macaroni* meant more than the now familiar tubular pasta. In 1760 a flashy group of Londoners who had traveled to Italy founded the Macaroni Club and introduced the new Italian food. They were a rakish group, devoted to gambling, drinking, and dueling, and so the name came to mean an affected dandy or fop, on both sides of the Atlantic. Indeed, during the American Revolution a Maryland regiment were known as the Macaronies for their showy uniform.

In mid-nineteenth century Britain *macaroni* was also pejorative slang for an Italian.

Macaronic verse, on the other hand, denotes poetry in which foreign words (often Latin) are distorted and jumbled in a humorous way. The term and the style both date from about 1500 in Italy, where *macarone* was a dialect word for a mixture of things, and were imitated in England and other countries. In 1520 a Mantuan monk published *Liber Macaronicum,* a poem made up of words in different languages and written in a comical style. This technique became popular enough so that by 1801 A. Cunningham could publish a history of macaronic poetry, *Delectus Macaronicorum Carminum.* An earlier example, dating from the fourteenth century, is the Christmas carol whose text combines German and Latin (the Latin is in italics) and which is still sung:

> *In dulci jubilo*
> Nun singet und seid froh!
> Leit *in praesepio.*
> Und leuchtet als die Sonne
> *Matris in gremio.*
> *Alpha es et O!*

Another kind of pasta, *spaghetti,* was so named when Marco Polo brought it to Italy from China in the early fourteenth century. Its name literally means "little strings," and indeed, in the fashion trade *spaghetti straps* are just that, narrow strips of fabric functioning as shoulder straps on a bare-shouldered bodice. To astronauts, however, a *spaghetti suit* denotes their long underwear, which is made up in part of tubes that carry cool water so as to prevent overheating when they are in orbit. This usage may have come from the *spaghetti* of electronics, where it denotes insulating tubing of small diameter into which thin wires can be slipped. *Spaghetti bender* is another pejorative name for an Italian, and a *spaghetti western* is a low-budget cowboy film shot in Italy or Spain, often using Italian actors and an American star, with the sound track dubbed into a single language. All these terms are of twentieth-century provenance.

A third kind of pasta, the *noodle,* is linguistically the most puzzling of the lot. The origin of the edible noodle appears to be German, with the word an anglicization of the German *Nudel.* But in colloquial English, "noodle" has several other meanings, and no one is sure how or if they are related to the pasta. One is *noodle* as a slang word for head and/or a silly or stupid person (sometimes called a *noodlehead*). Some experts theorized that this is really a variant of *noddle,* an older word for the head or brain, or perhaps even a portmanteau word combining "noodle" and "fool." This kind of noodle appears in the slangy *off your noodle,* meaning "off your head" or "crazy." Equally puzzling are the verb forms of *to noodle,* also put as *to noodle around,* which to musicians means to warm up or improvise a passage, in effect to fool around. To non-musicians it simply means to experiment, improvise, or freely devise, although William Safire holds it means to think over (*New York Times Magazine,* Sept. 22, 1991). And in Australia it has a more special meaning, that is, to mine opals.

SIX

Nuts to You

Botanically speaking, nuts actually are fruits, which in crude and offensive slang usage might be translated as "Crazy individuals actually are homosexuals."

The word *nut* for a hard or leathery shell surrounding an edible kernel has been around, in slightly different forms, for well over a thousand years. During that period, however, it also acquired various slang meanings, ranging from the now obsolete "thing of trifling value" (fourteenth century) to the still current "human head" (as in *off one's nut,* mid-nineteenth century) and "lunatic" or "crank" (early twentieth century). And in the plural, *nuts,* it acquired still more meanings, from "a source of pleasure and delight" (seventeenth to late nineteenth centuries; still current in Britain) to the vulgar slang name for "testicles" (early twentieth century) and as an expletive meaning "Nonsense" or "Rubbish" or a similar expression of disgust or defiance *(Nuts to you;* also twentieth century). These last usages are particularly interesting, because for a time, in the middle 1920s, saying "Nuts" was considered so vulgar (owing to the testicles meaning) that it was thinly disguised as *Nerts,* a euphemism that probably fooled no one. However, despite its widespread usage, censorship forbade uttering "nuts" in a motion picture—in 1941 Will Hays, then head of the Motion Picture Producers and Distributors of America and promulgator of the prohibitive Hays Code governing decency in movies, included it on a list of words to be omitted from American films.

Nuts and Nutty

To be nuts in the sense of being crazy (either mildly eccentric or actually suffering from severe mental illness) has been around since the mid-nineteenth century. The adjective *nutty* is used in the same way, as in *nutty as/nuttier than a fruitcake* (see NUTTY AS A FRUITCAKE). From these we have the equally slangy *nut house* for a mental hospital. Loosely related to these is the roughly contemporary *to be nuts about/on* something or someone, which, however, means to be "crazy about" or "enamored" or simply "very taken with" something or someone. Similarly, one might speak of an *exercise nut,* meaning an individual extremely enthusiastic about (or even obsessed with) physical exercise.

Why the edible nut (as distinct from the mechanical one in *nuts and bolts)* should give rise to so many colloquial meanings is hard to explain. Both the human head and male reproductive organs are roughly similar in shape to many kinds of nut, but other than that there is no clearcut relationship.

The physical characteristics of nuts are more aptly expressed in a *tough/hard nut to crack,* said of a difficult problem to solve or a hard person to deal with. Similar analogies were drawn from the sixteenth century or earlier, but the modern wording dates only from the mid-eighteenth century. Far older is the proverb *He who would eat nuts must first crack the shell*—that is, you must work in order to achieve something—which was already around in Roman times.

A more puzzling expression is *deaf nut,* a term used for something worthless or unsubstantial from the sixteenth to nineteenth centuries, as in "I live upon no deaf nuts" (Samuel Rutherford, letter, 1637). It rests on the older meaning of "deaf" as barren and unproductive and thus meant a nut that contains no edible kernel and, by extension, any empty or worthless enterprise.

And finally, we have *in a nutshell,* meaning a very concise summary. This phrase, still very current, dates from ancient Roman times, when Pliny described a copy of Homer's *Iliad* written in such tiny script that the entire long poem could fit into a nutshell. This early hyperbole caught the imagination of numerous later writers. Eventually the allusion to Homer was dropped and only the current expression remains.

Of the nuts used in cakes and other confections or eaten alone, the most important commercially are walnuts (including butternuts), pecans, almonds, cashew nuts, Brazil nuts, chestnuts, and filberts (also called hazelnuts). In contrast to the plain and simple nut, or the peanut (which isn't a true nut; see below), few of these varieties appear in other linguistic guises.

The almond gave rise to *almond-shaped* and *almond-eyed,* both alluding to the nut's narrow oval shape, tapered at both ends. The *butternut,* or white walnut, a native of North America, briefly gave its name to soldiers of the Confederate army, whose grayish-brown uniforms were dyed with an extract from the butternut tree.

Chestnuts

The *chestnut,* popular on both sides of the Atlantic until a severe blight virtually killed off these trees in North America, gave rise to two terms still current. *Pulling chestnuts out of the fire,* meaning to save the day (usually for someone else), alludes to the ancient fable in which a clever monkey persuades a cat to pull roasting chestnuts out of a fire in order to avoid burning its own paws. It has been used figuratively since at least the sixteenth century.

The origin of *old chestnut* for a stale, too often repeated story or joke, is more open to dispute. There are several theories about the source, the most likely of which is William Dimond's play *The Broken Sword* (1816), in which a character who constantly repeats the same story about a cork tree is interrupted by another who insists it is really about a chestnut ("I have heard you tell the joke twenty-seven times, and I am sure it was a chestnut").

Working for Peanuts

The most popular nut in America is the peanut. It actually is not a true nut at all, but the seed contained in an underground pod of a plant belonging, like peas, to the legume family. Peanuts are named for their resemblance to peas, although in Africa and other places they are known as *ground nuts.*

It is the relatively small size of peanuts, compared to other nuts, that has been linguistically transferred. Thus *working for peanuts* means working for very little pay, a term originating in the United States early in the twentieth century. *Peanut politicians* and *agitators* are mid-nineteenth-century Americanisms describing individuals addicted to mean-spirited, petty maneuvers; both these terms have died out. The *peanut gallery,* from late nineteenth-century America, survives. It originally meant the cheapest theater seats (bought for just peanuts), but was extended also to mean an unimportant source of criticism, that is, boos and hisses from the peanut gallery are worthless.

In the mid-twentieth century the American cartoonist Charles Schulz became famous for his comic strip *Peanuts,* drawn from 1950 on. It features the exploits of a group of youngsters (small fry, or "peanuts"), all members of Charlie Brown's baseball team, through which Schulz poked gentle fun at both juvenile and adult foibles. The characters—Charlie, his dog Snoopy, Snoopy's friend and confidant, Woodstock the bird, loudmouth Lucy, insecure Linus, tomboy Peppermint Patty, and Schroeder the pianist—have achieved worldwide popularity through syndication and animated cartoons on television.

SEVEN

Dairymaids and
Butter-and-Egg Men

Until not long ago, fried eggs, buttered toast, and a glass of milk were considered an excellent, wholesome breakfast. Only recently have dairy products and eggs gotten a nutritional bad name. Indeed, butter, cheese, cream, milk, and eggs were prized foods during those many centuries when we were happily ignorant of the deleterious effects of overindulgence in butterfat and cholesterol. Despite the dire warnings of contemporary nutritionists, these foods are enshrined in numerous linguistic transfers.

Butter Wouldn't Melt ...

An ancient legend has it that butter was discovered accidentally when an Asian horseman galloped across a plain on a hot day, carrying with him a goatskin filled with sour milk. When the rider stopped to drink his milk, he was amazed to find a golden substance in the bag. Tasting it, he found it delicious, and soon butter was being made in countless goatskins. The shaking method of making butter is still used in some parts of the world, but in most places it was quickly replaced by the butter churn, which agitates cream until butter is formed.

> *The King asked the Queen,*
> *And the Queen asked the Dairymaid:*
> *"Could we have some butter for*
> *The Royal slice of bread?"*
> —A. A. Milne, When We Were Very Young

Butter is fairly sticky, which of course is why it adheres well to bread. This quality also gave rise to the saying *sealed with butter* for something that was securely sealed and, by extension, a certainty. It appeared in John Heywood's 1546 proverb collection and several later ones, but is obsolete today. The same collections include the proverb *No butter will stick on his bread,* meaning more or less the opposite, that is, nothing is going right for him. This saying, too, is virtually obsolete, but its equivalent, *His bread always falls butter side down,* meaning he always has bad luck, has survived.

Another extremely old locution is *Butter wouldn't melt in his/her mouth,* which also appeared in Heywood's 1546 book. Originally it was applied exclusively to a woman so excessively demure that her demeanor aroused suspicion—meaning she was nowhere near as virtuous as she seemed. (The metaphor implied she was literally so cool that butter inside her mouth could not melt.) In time the term lost its gender connotations and was applied to both men and women, referring rather to hypocrisy, as in Samuel Butler's *The Way of All Flesh* (1903): "Nor did I like having to be on my best behaviour and to look as if butter would not melt in my mouth."

Two somewhat newer terms allude to different characteristics of butter. A clumsy individual who frequently drops things has, since the early nineteenth century, been called *butterfingers,* referring to the slippery, greasy nature of the spread. And about a century later in America, *butterball* began to be used informally for a chubby individual.

In verb form, *to butter* or *to butter up* has meant, since the seventeenth century, to flatter someone effusively. This idea that butter enhances plain bread is echoed in a number of other common phrases. *To know which side one's bread is buttered on* has meant, since the sixteenth century, to know where one's own interests lie, and the saying remains current. *To butter one's bread on both sides* means to be extravagant, and *to have one's bread buttered for life* means to be well provided for. The last two are heard less often today.

Today *bread and butter* describe something basic, such as a means of support or income, although we write a *bread-and-butter letter* as a thank-you note for hospitality. Earlier, however, *bread and butter* had numerous other meanings, among them childish (in Beaumont and Fletcher's 1625 play *The Humorous Lieutenant:* "Ye bread-and-butter rogues, do ye run?"), and concern or business (in Samuel Foote's *The Mayor of Garret,* 1764: "It is no bread and butter of mine").

Another, more recent pairing is *butter-and-eggs.* It appears as the name of several plants with flowers in two shades of yellow, the pale one of butter and the deeper one of egg yolks. The common toadflax, *Linaria vulgaria,* which grows wild in many gardens, is one such plant.

The term *butter-and-egg money* originally meant funds earned by the farmer's wife from the sale of home-churned butter and eggs laid by her chickens. It later was extended to mean, in effect, pin money, funds she could spend as she wished. A special usage, *big butter-and-egg man,* is thought to have been originated by Texas Guinan (1884–1933), a famous American nightclub hostess who in 1924 so introduced a big-spending stranger who refused to give his name but admitted that he was in the dairy business. (However, newspaper columnist Walter Winchell attributed the term to master of ceremonies Harry Richman and said the original butter-and-egg man was "Uncle Sam" Balcom, a New York grocer.) The term quickly was adopted for any prosperous person who came to town and freely threw his money around, especially one who risked investing large sums in a theatrical production or nightclub venture. The term gained further currency when it became the title of a song (1924) sung by Louis Armstrong, and then was used by George S. Kaufman for the title of a Broadway comedy in 1925.

Say Cheese!

Cheese—milk's leap toward immortality.
        —Clifton Fadiman, *Any Number Can Play* (1957)

Cheese is made from the solid constituents, or curd, of milk, which is separated from the watery part, or whey. In general, it is made by setting the milk and cutting, stirring, heating, draining, and pressing the curd. Depending on the kind of cheese, the curd either is used fresh, as for cottage cheese, or is allowed to ripen. During the ripening process, bacteria and molds are introduced into the curd to produce particular textures and flavors.

Cheese is a very ancient food, and there are numerous expressions involving the word, although their meaning in relation to the food is not always clear. Moreover, the same expression sometimes has quite different meanings in Britain and America. For example *cheesy,* literally meaning of or like cheese, is British slang for stylish or chic, whereas in America it means shoddy and shabby.

One of the oldest surviving phrases is *the moon is made of green cheese,* which dates from the early sixteenth century, and its meaning has not changed over the centuries, that is, an illustration of extreme gullibility (if you would believe that, you would believe anything). The actual analogy is unclear, although John Ciardi thought the moon resembled a wheel of aging cheese wrapped in cheesecloth and glowing slightly in a dark cellar. Another proverbial oldie is *as different as chalk from cheese,* an English proverb from the fourteenth century on. Alliteration is probably what has kept it alive, at least on the British side of the Atlantic.

Two cheese terms turn up in underworld slang. *Cheese it, the cops!*—that is, watch out, the police are coming—is a warning cry dating from early nineteenth century Britain, where "cheese it" translates to stop or be quiet. Most authorities believe that "cheese" here came from "cease." A more recent one is *cheese eater* for a police informer, which Eric Partridge suggested alludes to a rat (also meaning informer) that loves cheese.

Several other slangy British locutions have not caught on much in America. One is *hard cheese,* meaning tough luck, which dates from the mid-nineteenth century. "It's hard cheese for a man to owe everything to his father-in-law," wrote Elizabeth Banks (*Manchester Man*, 1876). Another is *the cheese*, meaning quite the thing, or hot stuff, from roughly the same time. The origin of this last usage, however, is disputed. Some think it comes from the French *chose* (*c'est la chose*, that's the thing); others believe it comes from the Hindi *chiz*, for "thing"; and still others think it comes from the Old English *chese*, meaning "choice." While these derivations may seem far-fetched, *big cheese* for an important person, used in both Britain and America, almost certainly comes from the Hindi *chiz*.

Say cheese is a phrase used since the 1920s by photographers on both sides of the Atlantic in trying to get their subjects to smile. Pronouncing "cheese" does in fact move the lips into a smiling expression.

Perhaps the most recent use of *cheese*, and one that may not survive, is that of 1990s teenagers and college students in the meaning of camp, kitschy, or extremely corny. It generally is applied to something outdated enough to be brought back and parodied, for example, a television series or popular music group of earlier (1970s) days.

(Also see *cheesecake*, under LET THEM EAT CAKE.)

The Cream of the Crop

Things are seldom what they seem,
Skim milk masquerades as cream.
　　　　　　　—W. S. Gilbert, *H.M.S. Pinafore* (1878)

The fact that cream, the fatty part of milk, rises to the surface when milk is allowed to stand, has given rise to a number of commonly used metaphors. "A new class finds itself at the top, as certainly as cream rises in a bowl of milk," wrote Ralph

Waldo Emerson in his essay on manners (1841). The *cream of society,* or *crème de la crème,* as the French put it, has meant the wealthiest and most socially prominent since the early nineteenth century.

Much earlier yet *the cream* of something meant the very best. John Ray's *English Proverbs* (1678) had *the cream of the jest*—the funniest of all, and even earlier Philip Massinger had "the cream of the market," meaning the best of the crowd *(The City-Madame,* 1632). And to *skim off the cream* has long been used figuratively to mean taking the best of something. Literally, what remains is *skim milk,* lauded by the health-conscious (it is fat-free) but not rich or desirable by other tokens, as pointed out by Gilbert in the quotation above.

Last One in Is a Rotten Egg!

Humpty Dumpty sat on a wall,
Humpty Dumpty had a great fall,
All the king's horses and all the king's men,
Couldn't put Humpty together again.
                                    —Nursery rhyme, c. 1803

Eggs turn up in a large number of common expressions and with a considerable variety of meanings. A few terms relate to the fact that the egg literally is the beginning or germ of something (a bird). Among these is Shakespeare's use of *egg* to mean a young, still undeveloped person; in *Macbeth* the murderers who have killed Macduff's young son by mistake say, "What, you egg! Young fry of treachery." Others, like the famous Humpty Dumpty rhyme, allude to the egg's fragility and indivisibility. It is the denial of the latter characteristic that gave rise to the British term *curate's egg* for something both bad and good. This expression actually originated in a *Punch* cartoon published in 1895, depicting a humble curate having breakfast with his august superior, the bishop. The caption reads:

"I'm afraid you've got a bad egg, Mr. Jones."

"Oh, no, my Lord, I assure you. Parts of it are excellent!"

The impossibility of making this fine distinction (clearly the whole egg was bad, not just part of it) out of sheer tact gave the language the term "curate's egg" for something partly good and partly bad, and by extension neither here nor there.

Good, bad, and rotten all have attached themselves to the egg. The term *bad egg* comes from mid-nineteenth-century Britain and denotes someone who turns out badly or disappoints in some way. "In the language of his class," wrote Samuel A. Hammett *(Captain Priest, 1855)*, "the Perfect Bird generally turns out to be 'a bad egg.' " In contrast, a *good egg* is a pleasant, trustworthy individual, an expression so used since about 1910. Spoiled or rotten eggs have a distinctive putrid smell, but this is not necessarily invoked in *last one in is a rotten egg,* which comes from the playground or schoolyard. This phrase is no more meaningful than similar exhortations to hurry up and join in a game or race.

A number of expressions allude to the fragility of eggs. Chief among them is *don't put all your eggs in one basket,* meaning don't risk all you have in a single speculation or enterprise. This cautionary proverb, invoking the risk of dropping the basket so that all the eggs break, may well be much older, but it first appeared in print in 1666 in Torriano's *Common Place of Italian Proverbs.*

To *walk on eggs* means to tread very lightly indeed. This expression dates from about 1600 and is still current, though it usually is put *as if/though walking on eggs.* On the other hand, one *cannot make an omelet without breaking eggs,* a truism if ever there was one. Allegedly Robespierre, of French Revolution fame, is credited with making this statement (c. 1790), but in French *(On ne saurait faire une omelette sans casser des oeufs);* he presumably was alluding to the excessive zeal of his fellows in overthrowing the French monarchy. However, this saying was already well known in France; some ascribe it to Napoleon.

Anyone embarrassed for saying something so obvious could be said to *have egg on his face* (but only much later, since this turn of phrase only came into wide use about the mid-twentieth century). This metaphor for having made a mess or gaffe may, John Ciardi believed, derive from the audience showing their dissatisfaction by pelting a performer with raw eggs and other garbage, but he cited no particular evidence for it.

A *hard-boiled egg* is one that has been cooked long enough so that its yolk and white solidify. Since the late nineteenth century this term, or *hard-boiled* alone, has been used informally for a tough, unsentimental individual.

> *The reason the Yankees never lay an egg is because they don't operate on chicken feed.*
> —Dan Parker, *Sports Illustrated,* Apr. 7, 1958

To lay an egg, meaning to fail, entered the American vernacular in the 1920s. The usage is somewhat puzzling, since a chicken might well regard laying an egg as a fine accomplishment. Nevertheless, *Variety,* the journal of American show business, ran the headline WALL ST. LAYS AN EGG on October 30, 1929, the day after the spectacular stock-market crash that ushered in the Great Depression.

Sucking eggs is a different thing altogether. It is the first step in creating a form of special folk art, the elaborate decoration of virtually intact but empty eggshells. The shell is prepared by poking holes in either end of a raw egg and then sucking (or blowing) out the contents, a technique perfected by country people many centuries ago. Hence we have the expression *Do not teach your grandmother to suck eggs,* said derisively to a person who is trying to advise or instruct someone already well versed in the subject. It dates from the late seventeenth or early eighteenth century.

In military jargon, *scrambled eggs* alludes to the elaborate decorations on the hat of a senior officer. Another expression that became popular in the military, specifically the armed forces of World War II, is *What do you want, egg in your beer?* This bit of slang for "What special treatment do you think you deserve?" was a common reply to any kind of griping, but its derivation is a mystery. Adding an egg to a glass of beer could hardly enhance the taste, although it has been suggested that it might be thought to have aphrodisiac properties.

Another term alluding to eggs as valuable is *nest egg,* a sum of money set aside for retirement or some special goal. It comes from the old practice of inducing a chicken to lay eggs by putting an artificial china egg in its nest. Presumably the nest egg grows, through additional savings and interest, just as the chicken increased its egg production.

Although the term *egghead* was first used in Britain merely to describe a bald person, it soon was extended to intellectuals, perhaps because baldness was associated with mental achievement. In the United States the term was popularized by newspaper columnist Joseph Alsop during the presidential campaign of 1952, when he so described Democratic candidate Adlai E. Stevenson. Stevenson was both bald and intellectual, but the term soon was broadened to include his supporters, and eventually anyone of intellectual attainment. A 1956 *Variety* headline proclaimed the marriage of playwright Arthur Miller to movie star Marilyn Monroe, EGGHEAD WEDS HOURGLASS.

The popular culinary combination of ham and eggs is transferred in golf, where *ham'n egg* means playing well with a golf partner because of complementary skills or offsetting luck. And a *fried egg* to golfers means a golf ball buried in the sand. In numerous sports *goose egg* denotes zero, at least in America; in cricket, Britain's national sport, it is *duck's egg,* now usually shortened to *duck.*

Finally, we have the ancient, oft-repeated if ungrammatical saying, *as sure as eggs is eggs,* which has meant a dead certainty since the late seventeenth century. And what, you might well ask, is so sure about eggs? Probably nothing at all, since this saying appears to be a corruption of the logician's assumption of identity, X is X. Say it aloud, and the origin becomes crystal clear.

A Tub of Lard

Falstaff sweats to death
And lards the lean earth as he walks along.
      —William Shakespeare, *Henry IV,* Part 1, 2:2

The noun *lard* has meant rendered pork or bacon fat since the fourteenth century. Lard long was widely used in cooking and baking, as well as a spread for bread. From it comes the verb *to lard,* literally meaning to enrich a lean meat with fat, and also used figuratively in the sense of enhancing or ornamenting something plain, as in, "His poetry is larded with classical allusions." It also gave rise to the noun *larder,* originally a storage place for cured pork (ham and bacon) and, especially, the fortifying fat derived from butchered hogs; today it is simply a pantry and, figuratively, any source of food.

Applied to humans, lard is always unflattering. The terms *lard-bucket* and *tub of lard* are slang for overweight individuals, as is the even ruder *lard-ass* for one with an especially well-padded backside.

Orthodox Jewish dietary laws forbid the use of pork and pork products like lard, as well as the consumption of dairy and meat products at the same meal (or even from the same dishes). From these prohibitions arose the use of rendered chicken fat for many of the same applications of lard—as a spread and in cooking. In German and Yiddish the name for rendered fat is *schmalz* or *schmaltz*. The latter not only entered the English language but gave rise to another usage, *schmaltzy*, for oversentimental, as in, "Those romance novels are too schmaltzy for words."

The Milk of Human Kindness

Yet do I fear thy nature.
It is too full o' th' milk of human kindness.
—William Shakespeare, *Macbeth,* 1:5

The first food of all mammals, including humans, milk has the longest history of any food. Records exist of cows being milked as early as 9000 B.C. The Bible contains many references to milk, one of the best known being that in the Book of Exodus, which describes "a land flowing with milk and honey" (3:8). Indeed, *land of milk and honey* still denotes a place where good things abound and, figuratively, Paradise.

A frieze found in ancient Ur shows a dairy scene from 3500 B.C., complete with milk containers and strainers, and in ancient Greece, Hippocrates recommended milk for medicinal purposes c. 500 B.C.

Shakespeare's metaphor for compassion and sympathy, quoted above, calls up the positive image of a mother nursing

her child. It appealed to numerous later writers, among them
Richard Sheridan, Edmund Burke, Thackeray, and Dickens, all
of whom used *the milk of human kindness* with the same
meaning.

> *. . . the air was soft as milk. Why milk, wondered Castang,
> and why is milk used for so many contemptuous expressions
> meaning soft and flabby; the French "soupe-au-lait" and the
> English milksop.*
> —Nicolas Freeling, *No Part in Your Death* (1984)

The image of milk as a toothless child's food has also given
rise to terms equated with weakness. *Milksop,* originally meaning a piece of bread soaked in milk and fed to an infant, has
been used figuratively for a weak, spineless, timid man since
Chaucer's time. A more recent term with the same meaning is
milktoast, dating from the early nineteenth century. *Caspar
Milquetoast* was such a character in a very popular comic strip,
The Timid Soul, by American cartoonist H. T. Webster, and became so widely known that milktoast in America is still often
spelled *milquetoast.* Similarly, *milk and water,* literally meaning
milk that has been diluted with water, came to be used figuratively for something insipid, feeble, or mawkish. It was so
used on both sides of the Atlantic from the late eighteenth
century on but is heard less often today.

A child's first teeth still are called *milk teeth.* They are tem-
porary and fall out to be replaced by permanent teeth. *Milk
leg,* on the other hand, is a painful swelling of the leg that can
occur after a woman gives birth. So called since the late nineteenth century because the skin over it is white, it is caused by
a thrombosis of the large veins in the leg.

The *Milky Way,* a galaxy that includes our solar system but
to the naked eye looks like a luminous band stretching across
the sky, has been so called for its resemblance to a streak of

milk since Roman times. The English word, a translation of the Latin *via lactea,* was in common use by Chaucer's time. A *buttermilk sky,* on the other hand, is a much more recent term describing a cloudy sky resembling the mottled appearance of buttermilk. *(Buttermilk* itself is a misnomer; it is the more or less sour milk that remains after the butterfat has been skimmed off.)

> *It's no good crying over spilt milk.*
> —H. G. Wells, *You Can't Be Too Careful* (1942)

Once milk has been spilled, it is virtually impossible to put it back in a container. Although this is just as true of any other liquid, it is spilled milk that became a metaphor for "what's done is done" by the early seventeenth century. "No weeping for spilt milk" appeared in James Howell's *English Proverbs* (1659) and numerous later collections, and the saying is still current.

Other old terms involving milk are scarcely heard today. The *milkmaid* and *dairymaid* were made obsolete by mechanical dairy equipment, and the *milkman* making deliveries in his *milk wagon* was replaced by newer, cheaper methods of distribution. The last, however, is recalled in the World War II locution *milk run,* a term first used by R.A.F. fliers to describe a regular sortie, flown day in and day out, much like a daily milk delivery. It was adopted in the U.S. Air Force as well, where it was sometimes called a *milk round,* and where *milk train* denoted an early-morning reconnaissance flight.

EIGHT

Other Fish to Fry

Fish and seafood have constituted an important source of protein all over the world for thousands of years. Perhaps even before hunting with clubs was undertaken, early humans could dig shellfish from the sand and swim out into shallows to catch fish by hand. Early cave paintings in France and Spain show men fishing with pole and string, or spearing fish with a long sharp stick. Nor was fish consumption confined to seacoasts, for lake and river fish also are consumed. Moreover, fishing is a sport and leisure pastime as well as an industry.

Small wonder, then, that fish should appear in numerous terms and sayings. A person out of his or her usual environment and consequently appearing ill at ease is said to be *a fish out of water,* a turn of phrase credited to St. Athanasius, who supposedly used it in the fourth century. It reappears in Chaucer's *Troilus and Cressida* (1374) and other early sources, and is still used today.

An individual who drinks a great deal, or drinks to excess, is said to *drink like a fish,* a term that probably originated in

the belief that fish, which breathe through their open mouths, are constantly drinking. It dates from the seventeenth century.

Most fish are cold-blooded animals (only a very few species are not), whence Shakespeare's turn of phrase, "It was thought she was a woman and was turned into a cold fish" *(The Winter's Tale,* 4:3). *Cold fish* is still used to describe an unemotional, hard-hearted individual, although this was not precisely Shakespeare's meaning.

To be good to eat, fish must be quite fresh, for they spoil rapidly. "Fish is worthless unless fresh," wrote Pontanus in his Latin proverb collection of 1778. This characteristic was transferred in several ways. *Fish begins to stink at the head* was pointed out in the sixteenth century and then used figuratively for a nation's upper classes or leadership. H. G. Bohn quoted it in 1860 and explained, "The corruption of a state is first discernible in the higher classes."

Fresh fish has scarcely any odor, but stale fish smells. Therefore, if fish smells, its freshness is questionable, whence the word *fishy* came to mean suspicious or dubious. "Fish is good but fishy is always bad," wrote J. G. Hollands *(Everyday Topics,* 1876), and by then numerous writers had used "fishy" in this way.

Before the days of modern refrigeration, each day's catch was sold in a market, often by the fisherman's wife. Eager to sell the entire catch before it went bad, she loudly hawked her wares, giving rise to the expression *fishwife* for a noisy, scolding, coarse-mannered woman.

> *Fish and chips endures as England's original hot fast food, a quintessential institution. More than nine thousand outlets . . . still dispense the vinegary fare, wrapped hot and salty inside folds of plain newspaper.*
> —William E. Schmidt, *New York Times,*
> March 9, 1993

Many consider *fish and chips*—fried fish and fried potatoes—England's national food. Fish-and-chips vendors often wrapped their wares in newspaper, giving rise to *fish-wrapper* for a newspaper. The term *other/bigger fish to fry* also originated in Britain, as a way of saying, I have other (and, by implication, better) things to do. It has been around since the mid-seventeenth century, and is used in America as well.

A Scottish custom gave rise to the phrase *a pretty/fine kettle of fish,* for a mess or unpleasant predicament. At the height of the salmon-fishing season, Scots traditionally hold a riverside picnic, itself called "a kettle of fish," where fresh-caught live salmon are thrown into a pot over an open fire to boil and then are eaten out of hand. Eating in this way is a messy process, whence the transfer of the term to any awkward predicament. Henry Fielding used the term figuratively in *Joseph Andrews* (1742), and it remains current, although it is heard more in Britain than in America.

Until relatively recent times, Roman Catholics were asked to abstain from eating meat on Fridays as well as on other special feast days, which came to be called *fish days.* In England, after Henry VIII broke with Rome and established the Church of England, Protestants abandoned this custom, and Roman Catholics in general were distrusted, as agents of a foreign power (the Pope). Thus, in the reign of Henry's daughter, Elizabeth I, *he eats no fish* became a way of saying someone was an honest man who could be trusted, because he was not a Papist. In 1564, however, Elizabeth decided to enforce Protestant observance of fish days in order to aid the fishing industry as well as to curb meat consumption (because grazing was using up too much land that could bear other crops), and the saying in time became obsolete.

The abundance, and consequent low cost, of fish no doubt helped to make it England's national dish. It is alluded to in another popular expression, *There's lots of good fish in the sea,* intended to comfort a person who loses one opportunity, lover, friend, etc. "The sea has fish for every man," George Pettie wrote in 1576, a term that has been used figuratively ever since, by such diverse writers as Thomas Fuller, Sir Walter Scott, Anthony Trollope, and Ogden Nash.

The Codfish Aristocracy

Oh, no doubt the cod is a splendid swimmer, admirable for swimming purposes but not for eating.
> —attributed to Oscar Wilde

The cod is one of the most important food fish. The origin of its name is uncertain, but it has nothing to do with the cod of codpiece, which comes from the Old English *codd,* for pouch or scrotum. For centuries the cod was prized not only as a food but for an oil extracted from its liver, which was used medicinally as a source of vitamins A and D. However, *cod-liver oil* is not particularly tasty, and so it became synonymous with disagreeable medications of any kind.

The consumption of cod somehow became associated with New England, evident in the ditty calling Boston the "home of the bean and the cod" (see BEANTOWN). John Ciardi believed the term *codfish aristocracy* originated there as a contemptuous term for those whose fortune was derived from commerce—"vulgar moneybags," one early writer put it—rather than from inherited money or some admired profession. However, the earliest appearances of this term in print quote a South Carolina senator (July 9, 1850) and a *New York Herald* news story (Dec. 15, 1852), indicating that it was not restricted to New England. It is rarely, if ever, heard today.

And then we have the Briticism *codswallop,* heard in such phrases as *a load of codswallop,* equivalent to "stuff and nonsense." According to Ebenezer Brewer, it originated from an 1875 invention by one Hiram Codd of a mineral water bottle with a marble stopper. *Wallop* being slang for fizzy ale, *Codd's wallop,* said Brewer, was a contemptuous term used by beer lovers for mineral water and other weak drinks, and later was extended to mean simply rubbish or nonsense. Another version held that the contents of Codd's bottles, filled with fizzy mineral water, were called Codd's wallop for their resemblance to ale. These stories are appealing but probably not true. The *OED's* first citation for codswallop is dated 1963, and its etymology is listed as unknown. But one thing seems certain: the term has nothing to do with the fish.

Slippery as an Eel

The eel, a freshwater fish, has a long, snakelike body with only tiny scales in its skin, which therefore appears to be quite smooth. When it is wet, it is indeed slippery, which gave rise to the simile *slippery as an eel,* used by Chaucer's time. It remains current. A Latin proverb, "You hold an eel by the tail," meant you have to hold on tight when dealing with a slippery individual.

The Greek playwright Aristophanes wrote "Fishing for eels," when he meant fishing in troubled waters *(The Knights,* 424 B.C.), but this metaphor has not survived. In America *eel* was at one time a nickname for a New Englander. Thomas Haliburton used it in *The Clockmaker* (1862): "The eels of New England and the corncrackers of Virginia." This usage, too, is obsolete.

Red Herring

The herring, one of the most important North Atlantic food fish, has been a valuable catch for hundreds of years. Numerous writers, from Rabelais to Robert Browning, have called the Atlantic Ocean a *herring pond.*

Because it is so prolific, swimming in shoals that number billions of fishes, it gave rise to such sayings as *Virtues thick as herrings.* Like most fish, herring die very quickly when they are out of water. This characteristic gave rise to the term *dead as a herring,* which Shakespeare and many others used to mean very dead indeed. However, they lend themselves to many kinds of preservation—pickling, salting, drying, smoking—a huge advantage in times preceding refrigeration.

Raw herring is silvery gray and, if fresh, has scarcely any smell. But smoked herring is a reddish brown in color and has a very strong smell. It therefore was used as a lure to train hunting dogs to follow a scent. This practice gave rise to a more nefarious one, the use of a red herring to divert pursuing hounds from their objective, such as following the trail of an escaping criminal. From this comes the figurative use of the expression *red herring* for a diversionary tactic, which dates from the nineteenth century.

Mackerel and Sardines

A few other food fish have given rise to linguistic transfers. A *mackerel sky,* with its detached masses of cloud, resembles the dappled skin of this fish. It usually signals the coming of rain, a fact observed as long ago as 1681 in a Yorkshire book on agriculture. *Holy mackerel,* an exclamation usually expressing astonishment or surprise, is hard to connect with the fish; it is probably a euphemism for "Holy Mary." *Salmon pink* is a pale orange-pink, resembling this fish's flesh.

Finally, we have the *sardine,* any of several small species of herring that are usually cured, preserved, and, in modern times, canned. It is not known which came first, the name of the island of *Sardinia* from the Greek and Latin names for the fish, or vice versa, but sardines abound in the Mediterranean (and many other seas). The principal expression involving the fish is *packed in like sardines,* meaning extremely crowded, for in cans sardines are jammed together very closely indeed. The term has been used for human crowds (and other tightly packed objects) since the late nineteenth century. *Sardines* is also the name of a children's party game in which one player, It, finds a good hiding place. The others count to 100, after which they look for It and, when they succeed, join him or her in the hiding place. Naturally this spot becomes packed with players, whence the game's name.

Bivalve Mollusks:
Clams and Oysters

I simply cannot imagine why anyone would eat something slimy [a clam] served in an ashtray.
> —Miss Piggy, *Miss Piggy's Guide to Life*
> *(as Told to Henry Beard)* (1981)

Clams are found buried in sand and are harvested by digging. This is the source of the common if anthropomorphic saying, *happy as a clam at high tide* (often shortened to *happy as a clam)*, for at high tide the sand is covered and clams cannot ibe dug. It also gave rise to the name *clam diggers* for pants that end at the knee and so avoid the risk of getting wet when engaging in this pastime.

Clams are eaten both raw, on the half-shell (the "ashtray" in the quotation above), or cooked in a variety of ways—steamed, fried, in a soup called clam chowder, etc. For the inexperienced, opening raw clams can be a daunting enterprise, for the shells of these bivalve mollusks are very tightly shut. From this characteristic comes the British expression *tight as a clam,* for penurious or tightfisted, as well as the verb *to clam up,* meaning to keep one's mouth shut.

Oyster, n. A slimy, gobby shellfish which civilization gives men the hardihood to eat without removing its entrails.
> —Ambrose Bierce, *The Devil's Dictionary* (1881–1906)

King James I of England is credited with being the first to say, "He was a brave man who first dared to eat oysters." Around his time people came up with the idea that one must eat oysters only in months with the letter *R* in their name, that is, from September to April. In late spring and summer they are unwholesome, a theory probably devised because in northern waters oysters spawn during the remaining months and therefore are not generally available at that time. Also, oysters spoil quickly in warm weather, and spoiled oysters can cause severe gastric distress. In any event, this idea is still adhered to by many people today, prompting Ogden Nash's verse, "I'd like to be an oyster, say / In August, June, July, or May" (*The Oyster*, 1931).

Oysters have been valued not only as a food but for the fact that they produce pearls, the product of an internal irritation. It is probably this characteristic that Shakespeare alludes to in *The world's mine oyster*, meaning the world is a place from which I can extract a profit. This expression continues to be so used, but actually is not precisely how it appeared originally. In the play *The Merry Wives of Windsor*, it is the bragging Pistol's answer when Sir John Falstaff turns down his request for a loan: "Why then the world's mine oyster / Which I with sword will open" (2:2), meaning he will extract profit by force.

> *Give me my scallop-shell of quiet . . .*
> *And thus I'll take my pilgrimage.*
> —Sir Walter Raleigh, *The Passionate Man's Pilgrimage*

The scallop is most distinctive for its ribbed shell, with about twenty ribs extending to the wavy outer edge. The only edible portion is the big muscle that opens and closes the shell's two halves. But it is the shell that entered the language. It became the emblem of St. James of Compostela, a Spanish town whose shores abound with this shellfish. Pilgrims to his shrine wore the shell on their hats to ward off evil. By the seventeenth century patterns resembling the shell's wavy edge were called *scallops* or *scalloping*, a usage that persists.

Crusty Crustaceans—
Crabs, Lobster, Shrimp

Just about all the terms involving crabs concern the animal's habits rather than its characteristics as a food. A crab has ten legs, which cause it to have a strange gait. It seems to move in all directions, sideways and backward as much as forward. "You can never teach a crab to walk straight forward," wrote the Greek playwright Aristophanes (*The Peace,* c. 421 B.C.). From this habit comes the word *crabwise,* for a kind of sideways motion, like that of someone moving through a crowd. It also accounts for the name *crab canon,* for a musical form in which the principal melody is repeated backward (with the notes in reverse order from the original statement).

In rowing, *to catch a crab* means to make a bad stroke so that the oar strikes the water hard on the backstroke.

The word *crabby* for ill-tempered comes not from the crustacean but from the sour crabapple.

Although these [lobsters] are delicious, getting them out of
their shells involves giving them quite a brutal going-over.
  —Miss Piggy, *Miss Piggy's Guide to Life*
  (as Told to Henry Beard) (1981)

Despite the fact that this North Atlantic crustacean consists of far more shell than meat and must remain alive until just before it is cooked, the lobster has been a prized food for centuries. Around the turn of the twentieth century the most elegant New York City restaurants, renowned for their gilded interiors and high-society clientele, were called *lobster palaces* for their fashionable late-night lobster suppers.

The lobster's shell, greenish-black when raw, turns red when cooked. This phenomenon gave rise to several locutions, the most common still current one being *red as a lobster,* used for at least four centuries. In the 1600s *lobster* became a colloquialism for British soldiers from various regiments who wore red uniforms, a usage that crossed the Atlantic during the American Revolution and occasionally replaced the more common "redcoats." This term is now obsolete, as is the expression *died for want of lobster sauce.* According to Ebenezer Brewer, this phrase, said of a person who suffers with a disproportionate severity from some trifling disappointment or slight, originated at the French court of Louis XIV. At a banquet for the king, Vatel, the chef, was informed that lobsters intended for a sauce had not been delivered. Considering himself totally disgraced, Vatel ran a sword through himself.

On the other hand, John Ciardi advanced numerous theories for the origin of a still current expression, *lobster shift.* Apparently this term began to be used by New York City newspapermen for the late-night work shift (2:00 to 9:00 A.M.). One theory is that calling someone a *lobster* was a common insult at this time, much as "turkey" is now, and that some newsroom boss, observing his crew come to work, said they looked like a bunch of lobsters (Ciardi suggests perhaps "boiled," or drunk). Another proposes that the crew stopped to eat at fish and lobster houses on the way to work, and a third is that they came to work at a plant near the waterfront just as fishing and lobster boats put out to sea. Ciardi himself prefers the story about newspaper mogul William Randolph Hearst saying that, alluding to their red noses (from drunkenness), they looked like lobsters. None of these theories has been verified, and the true origin remains unknown. Nevertheless, the term *lobster shift* continues to be used, along with "graveyard shift" and "dogwatch," for late work shifts.

The most popular seafood item in America is the shrimp. That is not necessarily true in other parts of the world. Two Chinese proverbs cited by William Scarborough in his 1875 collection have it otherwise: "When there are no fish in the river, shrimps are dear" (Scarborough suggests this can mean daughters are precious when one has no sons), and "Who cannot catch fish must catch shrimps."

Like lobsters, shrimps change color when they are cooked, from gray to pink, giving rise to *shrimp-colored* for a shade of bright pink. However, despite the fact that not all varieties of shrimp are tiny (witness the oxymoronic "jumbo shrimp"), the oldest and most common linguistic transfer of *shrimp* is to a diminutive person. Used by Chaucer, it remains current.

Caviar

The pickled and salted roe (eggs) of sturgeon has long been one of the world's most expensive luxury foods. At this writing top-grade caviar can cost as much as $400 a pound. Hence the very word became a symbol of luxury and cultivation, but an acquired taste, not necessarily appreciated by all. It was so used by Shakespeare in *Hamlet* (2:2):

> *The play, I remember, pleased not the million;*
> *'Twas caviare to the general.*

In other words, it did not appeal to the masses. H. H. Munro (Saki) played on Shakespeare's metaphor in *Reginald* (1904), "There are occasions when Reginald is caviare to the Colonel."

The caviar industry, incidentally, has long been cloaked in secrecy and intrigue. Mislabeling, using cheaper illegal compounds instead of sea water to cure the eggs, and tax evasion are common. Unscrupulous vendors frequently try to pass off the lowest and cheapest grades of sturgeon caviar as Beluga, the highest grade, or to represent domestic caviar as imported. The finest and costliest caviar comes from sturgeon in the Caspian Sea, with Iran and the former Soviet Union the chief producers. Sturgeon also are found in American waters, particularly in the Columbia River and the Missouri drainage from Mississippi to Tennessee, and as political upheaval diminished imports, the value of the American product rose. In colonial times, sturgeon was so plentiful in the Hudson River that it was called "Albany beef," and its caviar was served in saloons instead of the then much costlier peanuts. Those days are long gone. Today egg-harvesting is protected by strict laws that vary from state to state, and poaching has become an increasing problem.

Apart from caviar, more ordinary *fish eggs* also is a colloquialism for tapioca pudding, which it resembles.

NINE

One Man's Meat

"Much meat, much malady," wrote John Clarke in 1639 (*Paroemiologia*). This statement was not as prescient of modern health considerations as it might seem, for *meat* in his time not only signified the edible flesh of animals but was often a metaphor for food, much as bread is. So what Clarke probably meant, in an expression that entered numerous subsequent proverb collections, was that overeating is bad for you. (An even earlier statement of the modern nutritionist's point of view is Martial's epigram, "Meat is the thing if you want to be fat" [c. A.D. 85], but the Romans no doubt viewed fat as a more desirable condition than we do today.)

The same metaphor figures in the expression *One man's meat is another man's poison,* meaning what one person finds desirable and good may be anathema to another—there's no accounting for tastes. It dates from the early seventeenth century and has been repeated ever since. One twentieth-century writer even believed that it constitutes an early description of food allergy, a rather specialized interpretation.

An even older expression is *it is meat and drink to me*, which has signified life's essentials (food and drink) as well as a source of deep enjoyment since the sixteenth century. John Frith was among the earliest to use it, "It ys meate and drinke to this childe to plaie" (*A Boke Answering unto Mr. Mores Letter*, 1533), and it was repeated by Shakespeare and Robert Browning, among others. Eric Partridge deemed it a cliché by 1940.

The flesh of animals, or meat, was one of man's first foods, even before the discovery of fire and the virtues of cooking food. Ancient laws and writings are full of restrictions and regulations concerning the use of meat. The ancient Egyptians and Hebrews were not permitted to eat any part of the pig, and strict rules governed the consumption of other meats. The Romans did eat pork but were aware of the dangers of undercooking it. The Phoenicians ate no beef or pork but were fond of dog meat, as were some of the native American tribes.

As civilization progressed, meat animals were raised and bred and crossbred to develop better strains, but meat pro-

duction remained a family or local matter until the mid-eighteenth century. And not until the development of refrigeration in the nineteenth century could the production of fresh meat (as opposed to salted or otherwise preserved animal flesh) become a major commercial enterprise.

> *No deals. You know why? Because your client is dead meat—and all of us know it.*
>
> —Susan Isaacs, *Magic Hour* (1991)

To *make meat of* has meant to kill someone since the mid-nineteenth century, whence the slangy *dead meat* for someone doomed to ruin or defeat, or even death. The last is meant in the quotation above, whereas mere defeat is invoked in this *New York Times* article about the 1992 presidential campaign: "No one here believes that the Democrats will ever let Tsongas be the nominee anyhow. Once he goes South, he's dead meat" (Maureen Dowd, Feb. 16, 1992).

In the 1920s the American slang term *meat wagon* began to be used for an ambulance, and sometimes also for a hearse. A much older and more vulgar usage was *meat* for the penis, which dates from the sixteenth century and was so used by Shakespeare and others. It survives in the scatological twentieth-century term *beat the meat,* for male masturbation. Not quite as vulgar but still demeaning is *piece of meat* for either a strong physical specimen (construction worker, prizefighter, weight lifter, etc.) or an individual regarded mainly as a sex object. The latter is also alluded to in *meat market,* slang since the late nineteenth century for a human flesh-peddling enterprise such as a prostitutes' hangout. The word *fleshpot,* originally meaning simply a pot for cooking meat, has been extended in the same way. The word alone can mean a place offering unrestrained pleasure (as in *the fleshpots of the French*

Baloney!

Italians make fine sausages, and one kind, a seasoned cooked sausage, is named for the city with which it became identified, Bologna. In late nineteenth-century and early twentieth-century America, however, the spelling of the name was changed from *bologna* to *baloney* or *boloney* to correspond with the anglicized pronunciation of the word (all three spellings remain current), and it tended to be made of cheap meat scraps, hence becoming identified as an inexpensive luncheon meat. From this came the popular catch phrase *It's baloney, no matter how you slice it,* literally meaning, "It's of little value, no matter what," and soon used figuratively for "It's nonsense, bluff, or make-believe." The phrase became current about 1930, and one of Eric Partridge's correspondents suggested that it may have come from a jingle of that period:

> *Dress it in silks and make it look phony,*
> *No matter how thin you slice it, it's still baloney.*

Presidential candidate Al Smith used it in a campaign speech, and in a 1954 radio broadcast Bishop Fulton J. Sheen defined it, "Baloney is the unvarnished lie laid on so thick you hate it; blarney is flattery laid on so thin you love it."

The name of another originally Italian sausage, *salami,* occasionally is played on in the same way. Maxwell Anderson had it in his 1939 play, *Key Largo:* "Salami's salami whether it's in six cuts or five." Further, in late twentieth-century American slang, salami is used in a number of contexts to denote a little at a time, alluding to the sausage's being thinly sliced. For example, "He set up the trust like a salami," meaning the proceeds would be doled out only a little at a time.

Where's the Beef?

I am a great eater of beef, and I believe that does harm to my wit.

—William Shakespeare, *Twelfth Night*, 1:3

Beef, the flesh of cows, bulls, and steers raised for their meat, is closely associated with England, and consequently turns up in numerous common expressions. Indeed, *beefeater* is an informal term for an Englishman, as well as the name for the Yeomen of the English royal guard and warders of the Tower of London. It was Henry VIII who first formed the royal bodyguard so named, and Edward VI who appointed the Yeomen Extraordinary to be Warders of the Tower; the latter still wear the costume of the Tudor period. The appellation "beefeater," which dates only from the mid-seventeenth century, at first had a slightly different meaning. An older sense of "eater" was "servant," so beefeater meant "well-fed servant," a not inaccurate description of the elite royal guardsmen.

Beef was long considered an extremely healthful food, imparting vigor and strength. Broth made from beef bones (*beef bouillon*) was used as a tonic for those weakened by illness or for anyone who was deemed run down. The adjective *beefy* therefore meant brawny and, in the days before it was considered unhealthy, obese. A more recent usage is *to beef up* something, meaning to strengthen it; it dates from the mid-twentieth century (although in mid-nineteenth-century American college slang *to beef* meant to put on extra exertion). Another newer term is the informal *beefcake*, for photographs of young men that display their muscular physique; it is the male equivalent of cheesecake.

In 1984 the third-largest American hamburger chain, Wendy's, launched a television commercial in which three elderly ladies are presented with a substantial-looking hamburger in a restaurant called "home of the Big Bun." They admire the bun, which contains only a sliver of meat, but one of the ladies, a retired manicurist named Clara Peller, telephones the restaurant owner and angrily demands, *"Where's the beef?"* While this commercial may not have increased Wendy's market share appreciably, the slogan became a national watchword, used in the 1984 presidential campaign. It was most closely identified with former vice president Walter Mondale, who, seeking the Democratic nomination, used it to attack the emptiness of his opponents' stands and promises. (Mondale won the nomination but lost the election to Ronald Reagan.)

At least a fraction of the popularity of this phrase probably stems from its similarity to *what's the beef,* meaning what's the complaint. The verb *to beef* and the noun *beef* in the sense of gripe both originated as American slang in the 1880s, and the relationship to the meat is not altogether clear. Nevertheless, the usages crossed the Atlantic and remain current. A 1990s version of American street slang is *to have beef* with someone, meaning to have an argument or feud; this kind of *beef* is typically settled in a confrontation involving weapons.

Cold Shoulders, Tenderloins, and Other Cuts

Changing a live steer into cuts of beef involves about fifty operations. The carcass first must be thoroughly bled and then skinned. A cooling period of twenty-four to forty-eight hours follows before the carcass is divided into the standard cuts of beef. There are nine wholesale cuts in a side of beef: round, rump, loin end, flank, short loin, plate rib, brisket-shank, and chuck. From these some three dozen retail cuts are obtained, including the familiar steaks and roasts.

Several cuts have given rise to common words or phrases. *Chuck,* the cut of beef between the neck and shoulder blade of the steer, is thought by many to be the source of *chuck wagon,* American frontier slang for a wagon carrying food and facilities to cook it for cowboys, ranch workers, and others in the fields. (In Britain, however, the word "chuck" was mid-nineteenth-century slang or dialect for "food" or "grub," and the American word may have developed from this source.)

To *give someone the cold shoulder,* meaning to snub someone, is definitely of British origin, first appearing in nineteenth-century writings by Sir Walter Scott and others. It is believed to come from the custom of welcoming an honored guest with a meal of roasted meat, but serving only a cold shoulder of beef or lamb—that is, a far inferior dish—to those who outstayed their welcome.

The cut called *sirloin* comes from the upper part of the loin and was originally spelled *surloin,* the "sur" from the French for "upper." This derivation was either forgotten or ignored, and a famous spurious etymology was substituted. Thomas Fuller's account, in his *Church History of Britain* of 1655, is one of the oldest: "A Sir-loyne of beef was set before Him (so knighted, saith tradition, by this King Henry [VIII])." A century or so later Jonathan Swift credited King James I with the act of knighting the large loin of beef at his table.

The *tenderloin,* lying between the sirloin and the ribs, is one of the choicest and most expensive cuts. In the 1880s, therefore, its name was used for a New York City police district so known for vice and corruption that it was assumed heavy bribes allowed the police to afford such delicacies as tenderloin. Eventually the name Tenderloin was extended to any similarly corrupted urban district.

A Chicken in Every Pot

Until the late nineteenth century, America had no commercial poultry industry. Most people lived where they could keep a few chickens to provide meat and eggs for the family, with a little extra that could be sold to those who had none. Apparently this was not the case in Britain, where as early as the seventeenth century George Herbert's collection of prudent sayings had "The Chicken is the Country's but the City eateth it" (*Jacula Prudentum,* 1640).

When Henry IV was crowned king of France in 1589, he reportedly said, "I wish that every peasant may have a chicken in his pot on Sundays." Centuries later this dictum was picked up in America by Republican compaigners, who in 1928 urged voters to keep the ruling party in power because it had put *a chicken in every pot.* While Henry may have meant it literally, by 1928 the term simply was a metaphor for the prosperous boom that preceded the Great Depression of the 1930s.

As individuals who are likely to go on lecture tours to promote their ideas, politicians are also among those responsible for two more recent coinages, the *chicken-à-la-king and mashed-potatoes circuit* and the *chicken-patty circuit.* Both Americanisms dating from the mid-twentieth century, these mildly disparaging terms describe the fare frequently served by clubs to their guest speakers.

Chicken has been slang for a girl or young woman since the early eighteenth century, and by the early nineteenth century in America a woman no longer young was described as *no chicken.* By 1900 this last expression was modified to *no spring chicken,* a sobriquet that actually makes no sense, for in poultry farming it is the young males, or cockerels, born in spring, that customarily were sent to market in fall as "spring chickens."

Two other expressions deserve mention, although they are

more concerned with raising chickens than eating them. One is the age-old riddle, *Which came first—the chicken or the egg?*, which has become a metaphor for sorting out causes and effects. The other is the cautionary proverb *Don't count your chickens before they hatch*, based on Aesop's fable of the milkmaid daydreaming about the profits from her milk (to be sold for eggs hatching into chickens) so that she spills her pail of milk. It, of course, remains a metaphor for spending one's profits before they are earned.

Sauce for the Goose

Who eats goose on Michael's-day
Shan't money lack his debts to pay.
                              —*The British Apollo* (1708)

In Britain roast goose has long been traditional fare for Michaelmas (St. Michael's Day, September 29). In France, on the other hand, it is traditional to eat goose on St. Martin's Day (November 11), because supposedly St. Martin was so annoyed by a goose that he ordered it slaughtered and served for dinner.

To *cook someone's goose* has for centuries been used in the sense of sealing someone's doom, but the true origin of the expression is not known. The most persistent theory has it that the defenders of a town under siege hung out a goose from its wall in defiance of the enemy, who in turn became so angry that they burned the town and, along with it, "cooked" the goose. Another version has the farmer slaughtering the fabled goose in order to get at its golden eggs, thereby doing away with his source of wealth.

What's sauce for the goose is sauce for the gander dates from the seventeenth century (it was already a proverb in John Ray's 1670 collection) and generally is used to mean what's good for one is good for another of the same kind. An earlier version, in John Heywood's 1546 collection, had it as *what's good for the cow calf is good for the bull,* but it is the goose that survived, and the saying has numerous variants (such as: *what's good/fair/ for goose is good for gander; what's wrong for goose can't be right for gander; as is gander, so is goose).* However, one writer qualifies it, at least from a culinary standpoint. "What is sauce for the goose may be sauce for the gander," wrote Alice B. Toklas, "but is not necessarily sauce for the chicken, the duck, or the guinea hen" (*The Alice B. Toklas Cookbook,* 1954). See also under SAUCES.

Ham It Up

> *Like a strutting player, whose conceit lies in his ham-string . . .*
> —William Shakespeare, *Troilus and Cressida,* 1:3

Ham is the upper part of a hog's rear quarters, and although it is sometimes sold as fresh meat, it most often is available salted and smoked. Transferred to another part of the body, it gave rise to *ham-handed* and *ham-fisted,* both meaning clumsy and heavy-handed; presumably the words allude to hands similar in shape to a ham.

Several theatrical terms allude to ham, but their origin is even murkier. A *hambone* was, in mid-nineteenth-century American vaudeville, a white actor masquerading as a black minstrel, that is, made up in blackface and using a sort of black dialect. Later in the century the term was used for an inferior actor, similar to the current usage of *ham,* whose origin has long been disputed.

In Shakespeare's day, the word "ham" referred not to the upper thigh or buttock, as it does today, but to the hollow or bend of the knee, and the *hamstring* then meant the large tendon behind the knee (as it does today). Some authorities believe the modern use of *ham* for a performer who overacts *(hams it up)* is a shortening of hamstring as used in the quotation above. Others also ascribe it to Shakespeare's time but believe it alluded to actors who performed his play *Hamlet* badly, or who had fallen on bad times but had appeared in *Hamlet* in better days.

Both theories are appealing but do not explain why the usage did not surface until the mid-nineteenth century. A more likely explanation of the source, therefore, is that it is an abbreviation of *hamfat,* a nickname for lard, which actors used to remove makeup. A popular black minstrel song of the 1880s, *The Ham-Fat Man,* probably helped the term gain currency, and by 1900 or so it was shortened to *ham.* Sylva Clapin's *A New Dictionary of Americanisms* (1902) had two definitions for ham, sporting slang for a loafer and, in theatrical parlance, a tenth-rate actor or variety performer.

The use of *ham* for an amateur radio operator dates from the 1920s and originally alluded to their lack of skill. That connotation has been lost, but the usage is still current.

Hot Dog!

The noblest of all dogs is the hot-dog; it feeds the hand that bites it.
—Laurence J. Peter, *Quotations for Our Time* (1977)

Although hot sausages in rolls or buns were being sold by American street vendors in the nineteenth century, it was not until 1900 that they were dubbed *hot dogs.* According to an apocryphal story, food concessionaire Harry Mozely Stevens was the first to sell them at the Polo Grounds ballpark, home of the New York Giants. Because of their Germanic origin (the sausages had long been called "frankfurters" after their hometown) and their resemblance to the short-legged, long-bodied German breed of dog called dachshund, he called them "hot dachshund sausages." But sports cartoonist T. A. Dorgan, who signed his work *TAD,* decided that this name was too long or too hard to spell and changed it to "hot dogs."

However, the name "hot dog" may have originated much earlier, in the mid-nineteenth century, in humor about sausages being made from the meat of dogs, cats, horses, or even rats (according to sociologist Irving Lewis Allen). It may have begun in a much publicized scandal over dog meat being served. Further, German immigrants jokingly called frankfurter sausages *Hundewurst* (dog sausage), which gave the name further impetus. The association with dog meat put the name into disrepute for a long time (in 1913 Coney Island merchants were forbidden to use it), but by 1939, when President Franklin D. Roosevelt and the visiting king and queen of England sampled it publicly, it again became respectable.

Basic American cookout and baseball fare, the hot dog has been transferred in at least two ways. "Hot dog" was 1890s' slang for good, superior, or the best, which may be why the exclamation *Hot dog!* became an expression of delight. It is sometimes embellished to *Hot diggity-dog!*

The verb *to hot-dog,* used since about 1960, means to show off, particularly in the sports of skiing and surfing, by performing extraordinary and dangerous stunts and maneuvers. A *Boston Globe* headline FRANKLY, FILMMAKER WOULD PREFER LESS HOT-DOGGING (Nov. 21, 1991) appeared over a story about a filmmaker's efforts to make a documentary about skiing, which were hampered by extreme leaps, flights and crashes of hot-dogging athletes.

Kidneys and Other Shapes

Organ meats such as beef or lamb kidneys are less popular in America than in Britain and other countries. Just about the only common linguistic transfer of the kidney in America is *kidney-shaped,* describing an oval shape indented at one end. It appeared in Britain in the eighteenth century but only became widely used in America in the twentieth century, for such objects as a kidney-shaped swimming pool. (The *kidney bean* also is so called for its shape.)

In Britain, however, the word *kidney* has been used metaphorically since Shakespeare's day for a person's temperament, and sometimes also for social class. "A man of my kidney" thus can mean either, depending on the context.

Another organ meat, liver, is probably as popular in America as in Britain. Long before its physiologic functions were understood, the term *liverish* meant resembling the reddish-brown color of liver and also having a disagreeable disposition, both crabby and melancholy. Further, the term *liver spots* has been used since the late nineteenth century for chloasma, a skin condition characterized by brown spots resembling the color of liver.

In Britain butchers and their customers differentiate between *lamb* and *mutton,* the latter denoting meat from mature sheep (as opposed to young lambs). While this distinction is rarely made for the meat in America, two nineteenth-century terms involving mutton were nevertheless adopted. One is the *leg-of-mutton sleeve,* whose triangular shape resembles a leg of lamb. The other is *muttonchop whiskers,* for roughly triangular side whiskers, narrow at the temples and broad at the jawline, where they end (the chin is shaved). Both styles have gone out of fashion, but the terms remain. (One other, *muttonhead,* an eighteenth-century slang term for a dolt that is occasionally still heard today, does not allude to the meat but to the sheep's stupidity.)

Still another fashion no longer current is the *sausage curl,* a lock of hair formed into a thick curl, as thick as a sausage. So called since the early nineteenth century, it was still being described in hairdressing manuals of the 1960s.

I'll Settle His Hash

hash, x. There is no definition for this word—nobody knows what hash is.
—Ambrose Bierce, *The Devil's Dictionary* (1881–1906)

Hash is the thrifty cook's solution for leftovers—a dish made of chopped-up leftover meat, potatoes, and sometimes also vegetables, mixed together and pan-fried. Hash is not a noble food, so the term *hash-house* means a less than elegant restaurant, such as a diner, and a *hash-slinger* is a waiter, waitress, or short-order cook in such an establishment.

From the recipe for *hash* it is easy to see how the word has been transferred to something reused (Andrew Marvell had "the cold Hashes of plain repetition" in his 1672 play, *The Rehearsal Transposed)* or a messy mixture (Alexander Pope's "The hash of tongues a Pedant makes," in *Satires of Donne,* 1735), or simply a muddle. These senses also exist in various verbal locutions: *to make a hash of something,* meaning to make a mess, or bungle, or botch; *to hash over,* to bring points up again in a lengthy discussion; and *to rehash,* to reconsider.

And finally, from the early nineteenth century, we have *to settle someone's hash,* meaning to deal harshly with someone, to get rid of or subdue. Another expression with exactly the same meaning is *to make mincemeat of* something or someone. Mincemeat is a mixture of finely chopped ("minced") suet, organ meats such as beef heart, nuts, and fresh and dried fruits (raisins, currants, citron, etc.), used to fill a pie *(mince pie* is a traditional Christmas dessert on both sides of the Atlantic). But to make mincemeat of someone has been a metaphor for destruction since the seventeenth century.

Pork Barrel Legislation

Pork is perhaps the most important meat, pigs having been raised for that purpose long before beef cattle. Probably because it is so fatty, in nineteenth-century America *pork* became a slang term for financial profit, particularly among politicians, who used it specifically for federal funds awarded to particular localities or individuals as repayment for their support.

Pork used to be stored in barrels, and *pork barrel* similarly came to mean a source of wealth. By extension, *pork barrel legislation* came to mean laws passed to benefit a particular constituency and thereby ingratiate legislators with those voters.

Likewise, the term *pork-chopper* does not allude to that meat cut's shape but to its fattiness; the term means a labor official who is put on a union payroll not for his or her ability but as a reward for past services. The same word is also used for public officials and legislators who are primarily interested in personal gain and power. These Americanisms both date from the 1940s.

Meat pies are a staple of the British diet. A popular variety is the *pork-pie,* minced pork inside a piecrust. In the nineteenth century this name also began to be applied to a snap-brimmed hat with a round, flat crown that resembled the meat pie; the style was at first worn by women and later also by men. In mid-twentieth-century Britain, *pork pie* and *porky pie* also became Cockney rhyming slang for "a lie," or rather, this already existing usage gained currency through a popular television comedy series, *Minder,* set in working-class London.

Tripe

> This book . . . very vulgar . . . is a dish of literary and artistic "tripe-and-onions."
>
> —*The Spectator,* Dec. 24, 1892

Tripe, the first and second divisions of the stomach of a ruminant (ox, cow, sheep, etc.), is a variety meat consumed more in other countries than the United States or Canada. "The taste of tripes did seem so delicate to the Romans that they often killed Oxen for the Tripes sake," wrote Moufet and Bennet (*Health's Improvement,* 1655), and "Tripe's good meat if it be well cleaned" appears in John Ray's *English Proverbs* (1678). Nevertheless, both the word *tripe* and *bag of tripe* also were contemptuous epithets for a person by the late sixteenth century.

In the late nineteenth century *tripe* also was being used in the sense of trash or rubbish, particularly for written or spoken words of inferior quality. And this meaning survives today.

TEN

Not by Bread Alone

The word *bread* today describes a large variety of grain-flour products that are made into dough and baked. In the Western world, wheat is the grain most frequently used for bread, whereas in many parts of Asia rice is the most important grain.

There are two principal kinds of bread, yeast bread and quick bread. The former uses yeast as the leavening agent, which acts fairly slowly. Quick bread is leavened with baking powder, baking soda, or an acid such as sour milk, which act faster. *Unleavened bread* is made of flour and water without a leavening agent, and is solid instead of porous. In the Bible "unleavened" signified "pure"—that is, with nothing added—and on holy days Jews still eat an unleavened bread called *matzoh*.

There are almost as many kinds of bread as there are countries in the world. In northern Europe rye bread is preferred. The French and Italians eat a crusty white bread. The people of Spain and Latin America have the tortilla, an unleavened bread made of either wheat or corn flour. In addition, there are numerous specialty breads such as biscuits.

The Staff of Life

> *God maketh the staff of life whereon men live.*
> —From *The Book of the Dead:*
> *Hymn to Amen-Ra* (c. 4000 B.C.)

That bread is a basic food, a staff or support of life, was already observed in Egyptian times and repeated in various books of the Old Testament (Isaiah, Ezekiel, Leviticus, Psalms). The Bible also uses *to break bread* in several senses. In the Old Testament it means to break it for oneself or for others (to share it), and it may signify actual bread or other food. In the New Testament it acquires a special figurative meaning derived from Jesus's last meal with his disciples, that is, it signifies the sacramental bread of Communion (where bread stands for Jesus's body and wine for his blood).

Also in the New Testament, the Gospel of Matthew contains what became known as the Lord's Prayer, which includes the sentence *Give us this day our daily bread.* In later years, the meaning of *daily bread* was extended from daily food to basic sustenance, and eventually to one's livelihood (the earnings that sustain life). In eighteenth-century Britain, to be *out of bread* was slang for being out of work, and by the early nineteenth century the word *breadwinner* signified wage earner, as it still does.

Indeed, the equation of bread and wages is far older than the twentieth-century American slang usage of *bread* for money. "The finest poems of the world have been expedients to get bread," wrote Ralph Waldo Emerson in his journal in 1834, and money is clearly what he meant.

On the other hand, the Bible also warns that *Man doth not live by bread alone* (Deuteronomy 8:3), a caution repeated in the Gospel of Matthew. Here bread does not mean just subsistence food but material wealth. Virtually the same is meant by *Cast thy bread upon the waters, for thou shalt find it after many days* (Ecclesiastes 11:1). However, this particular metaphor for abandoning all material goods for spiritual rewards—which doesn't make much sense unless you interpret "bread" as "seed" thrown on floodplains that will take root and grow when the waters recede—today is thought to mean that a good deed will eventually bring you a reward.

Bread and Roses

There are numerous pairings involving bread. *Bread and butter* signifies a basic issue (see under BUTTER). *Bread and water* denotes the minimal fare needed to stay alive, constituting punishment for a prisoner or subsistence food for a penitent.

Bread and roses, however, signifies a chapter in the history of the American labor movement. On January 12, 1912, workers in the textile mills of Lawrence, Massachusetts, walked off the job to demand higher wages and more reasonable hours. Many of them were Italian immigrants who used the phrase *Pan' e rose* (Italian for "bread and roses") to symbolize both life's necessities and its pleasures. After a group of women strikers picketed with a banner that read, "We want bread and roses, too," *bread and roses* became a rallying cry for the strikers' demands for both a living wage and a better quality of life.

After two intense months, fraught with violence, the strikers won their demands, not only for themselves but for the entire textile industry. The concessions granted included both better working conditions and better wages. Soon afterward the phrase "bread and roses" was used in a poem by James Oppenheim, and later it appeared in folk songs about the labor movement, popularized by such singers as Mimi Farina and Judy Collins. By the early 1970s it was also adopted by the feminist movement, which named its first "liberation cell" Bread and Roses.

From roughly the same period as the Great Textile Strike, as it was called, came another American phenomenon, the *bread line*. Like the soup kitchen (see SOUP), it is a charitable enterprise in which the indigent are given food, at first literally bread but later extended to other handouts as well. In the 1890s Louis Fleischmann, owner of the Vienna Model Bakery in New York City, began handing out day-old bread to the needy. The line formed at midnight at the bakery's side door and extended for several blocks. It helped establish both the word "breadline" and the practice. Fleischmann's breadline was described by name in Theodore Dreiser's novel *Sister Carrie*. However, the word's first appearance in print occurred two decades earlier, in Albert Bigelow Paine's 1899 novel, *The Breadline: A Story of a Paper*. Much later, bowlers adopted the term "breadline" to signify the situation where a number of pins are left in a line (1–2–4–7 or 1–3–6–10).

The precise event that had triggered the Great Textile Strike was a law passed by the Massachusetts legislature that limited the workday to ten hours (it had been as much as sixteen). In response the mill owners lowered the daily wage considerably, a move that angry workers described as *taking the bread out of our mouths*. This turn of phrase originated about 1700. It first appeared in Motteux's translation of Rabelais's works, apparently as the translator's own interpolation. It is still used today to signify depriving someone of their livelihood.

A quite different idea is conveyed by a much older pairing, *bread and circuses.* Writing scornfully of the decline of Rome, where the people once took an avid interest in government, Juvenal said that today the populace cared only for two things, *Panem et circenses* (bread and circus games)—that is, food and entertainment. Later the term came to be used more loosely to mean any kind of crowd pleaser, particularly one offered by the government.

A *breadbasket* literally is a basket, bowl, or plate that contains bread and/or rolls. Figuratively, however, the word is used in a number of ways. Since the mid-eighteenth century it has been slang for a person's stomach or abdomen. From the early twentieth century on it has been used to describe a large agricultural area, particularly one known for grain production. Countries such as Hungary used to be called *the breadbasket of Europe,* and in America states such as Iowa are described as *a breadbasket state.* In bowling a *breadbasket* denotes a leave of 2–4–5–8 or 3–5–6–9 (that is, those pins remain standing).

A Baker's Dozen

In earlier times bread was sold by weight, and in Britain a severe penalty devolved on bakers who short-weighted their customers. Therefore it became the custom for bakers to sell thirteen loaves for the price of twelve, whence the term *baker's dozen* for thirteen. (The *OED* offers another explanation: dealers purchasing their bread from bakers were entitled by law to receive thirteen loaves for the price of twelve, the thirteenth loaf representing their cut of profit.)

Another equally old saying is *Half a loaf is better than none,* a truism that appeared in John Heywood's *Proverbs* (1546) and numerous other sources. It continues to be used to mean something is better than nothing, even if it is not all you expected or desired.

Of more recent and American provenance is *sourdough bread,* a staple of pioneering days in the Old West and today considered a northern California specialty. It is bread leavened with a sourdough starter, which originally was a simple combination of milk and flour kept in a warm place until it began to bubble from the activity of bacterial fermentation. Only a portion of the starter was used for each batch of bread, and it was immediately replenished with additional milk and flour. It is said that throughout the West the zesty sour aroma floated from starter crocks everywhere—chuck-wagon larders, homesteaders' kitchens, covered wagons, miners' tents. Old starters were carefully guarded and shared with family and friends, and some strains were said to be more than thirty years old. From this practice the word *sourdough* became American slang for a prospector, a miner who lives alone or with a partner and eats bread of his own making. A 1907 folk song collection by Robert W. Service was entitled *Songs of a Sourdough,* but this usage has largely died out with other folk ways of the Old West.

Bread that must be sliced with an axe is bread that is too nourishing.

—Fran Lebowitz, *Metropolitan Life* (1978)

As commercial baking became more automated, bread took on the anonymity of many factory products, at least in North America. ("You can travel fifty thousand miles in America without once tasting a piece of good bread," wrote expatriate Henry Miller in *Remember to Remember,* 1947.) Huge machines, largely automated, measure, mix, divide, knead, and perform all the operations required to produce uniform loaves of sliced white bread in sanitary wrappers—the kind that still accounts for most of the bread sold. Alluding to the convenience of such food is the hyperbole *best/greatest thing since sliced bread,* said either approvingly or sarcastically of a new invention. It is thought to have originated in the American armed forces in the mid-twentieth century.

At the same time, white bread has acquired a bad name, and not just among dieticians, who complain it is so over-refined that it has no nutritional benefits. Following the defeat of President George Bush in the 1992 election, one of his friends explained his loss to a *New York Times* reporter: "He was only comfortable with a damn white-bread crowd, a bunch of white male Protestant number-crunchers and bean counters" (quoted in the *Boston Globe).* But, the *Globe* editorial continued, the United States has never been a white-bread country—it is made up of numerous nationalities and races. *White bread* here signifies a homogeneous white establishment and implies the exclusion of other ethnic and racial groups.

Another less than flattering usage involving bread is *pap,* which literally means a soft food made of bread soaked in milk or water, fit for infants and invalids. (See also MILKSOP.) In nineteenth-century America the word came to signify political patronage, the bestowal of office on someone as a reward for support. This usage is obsolete, but in the twentieth century *pap* began to be used for an idea, book, play, or the like that lacked real value or substance, as in, "To describe this record as 'maudlin pap' must be extremely hurtful ..." *(Sounds,* Dec. 11, 1976; cited by the *OED).*

Bagels and Pretzels

The bagel [is] an unsweetened doughnut with rigor mortis.
—Beatrice and Ira Henry Freeman,
New York Times, May 22, 1960

A firm-textured, ring-shaped roll made of leavened dough that is briefly poached in water to give it a hard sheen before it is baked for a chewy interior, the *bagel* originated as a Jewish food but by the 1990s had become popular throughout the United States. In effect, it played the same role as the south Italian pizza had done some decades earlier. As "bagelmania" swept the country, bagels, like pizza, became available not only fresh but frozen, enabling extremely widespread distribution.

The word "bagel" is thought to come from the German *Beugel,* in turn originating from a diminutive of bracelet or ring. In Yiddish it is spelled *beygl* and first appeared in print in 1610 in the communal rules of Cracow's Jewish community, which stipulate that bagels are among the gifts that may be given to women in labor and to midwives. However, this source does not describe just what a bagel is, so its exact origin remains a matter of dispute. Indeed, one theory is that it was invented by a Jewish baker in Vienna in 1683 to thank the king of Poland for protecting his country against the Turkish invaders. The baker shaped the roll in imitation of a riding stirrup (in German, *Bügel*) to honor the king's favorite pastime, riding horses.

Whatever the origin, the bagel caught on and followed East European Jews to America around the turn of the twentieth century. New York City in particular became home to bagel bakeries, and according to one source, it was easier to get into medical school than to get an apprenticeship in one of the thirty-six union bagel shops in New York City and New Jersey.

In the 1970s, two professional tennis players who also happened to be Jewish became known for frustrating their opponents in seemingly endless rallies with their slow, high-looping strokes. One of them, Eddie Dibbs, coined the term *to bagel,* meaning to win a game or set so overwhelmingly that the opponent's score was 0 (his term obviously alluded to the hole in the bagel). Soon afterward a sportswriter, Bud Collins of the *Boston Globe,* called him and his friend, Harold Solomon, the *Bagel Twins,* alluding to their similar style of play. The two players have long since retired from tournament competition, but the verb "to bagel" was adopted in other sports as well with the same meaning.

Paul Dickson also cites *bagel* as automotive slang for a poorly maintained car, so called by an individual considering it for a trade-in, but gives no citations for this usage.

Like the bagel, the *pretzel* is European in origin. Its name is an anglicization of the German *Brezel* or *Bretzel,* but pretzels are found in numerous European countries. There are many kinds of pretzel—large and small, sweet and savory—but all with the same characteristic shape: a rope of dough formed into a loop, with an extra twist given to the ends. (The German word comes from the Italian *bracciatello,* a ring-shaped bun, in turn derived from the Latin *bracellus* for bracelet. At least one pretzel expert believes a pretzel is always pictured with the tips pointing up in unconscious recognition that it represents the human shoulders with arms folded.) Europeans enjoy sweet buttery pretzels fragrant with nuts, spices, or chocolate, large coffee-cake pretzels made from a yeast dough, as well as the kind most familiar in America, crisp salted beer pretzels brought by German immigrants. (The name of the fat, crunchy *Dutch* pretzel is a corruption of *Deutsch,* meaning "German.")

It is the pretzel's odd shape that has been linguistically transferred. Squeezing yourself into a small, awkward space, you might describe your contorted form as resembling a pretzel. For the same reason, musicians use *pretzel* as slang for the French horn, with its numerous twists, and the related *pretzel bender* for a French horn player.

Biscuits

The word *biscuit* comes from Latin words meaning "baked twice," and was spelled "bisket" in England from the sixteenth to eighteenth centuries. The current spelling was adopted from the French for "twice-cooked" but was always pronounced like the earlier spelling, which, the *OED* complains, makes no sense. Presumably biscuits were at one time baked twice, making them crisp and hard and long-keeping, ideal for travelers, sailors, and others undertaking a long voyage.

Today, the word has different meanings in Britain and America. The British biscuit is an unleavened wafer, what Americans call a *cracker,* although *sweet biscuit* is what Americans call a *cookie.* The American biscuit, a soft roll leavened with soda or baking powder, is called a *scone* in Britain.

The British biscuit tends to be light brown in color, giving rise to both *biscuit color* for this shade and *biscuit ware* for pottery that is left unglazed (the latter is sometimes called *bisque ware*).

Buns, Etc.

Now for the tea of our host,
Now for the rollicking bun,
Now for the muffin and toast,
Now for the gay Sally Lunn!
            —W. S. Gilbert, *The Sorcerer* (1877)

Today the word *bun* signifies any of numerous kinds of bread roll, usually leavened with yeast. Nobody is sure exactly where the word originated, but many people think it is derived from the Old French *bugne,* for a swelling. One kind of bun, called a *Hot Cross bun,* is a special food for Good Friday. It was supposed to be made of the dough kneaded for Communion bread and marked with a cross on top. This kind of bun allegedly keeps for twelve months without growing moldy. *Poor Robin's Almanack* (1733) described it:

Good Friday comes this month: the old woman runs.
With one a penny, two a penny "hot cross buns,"
Whose virtue is, if you believe what's said,
They'll not grow mouldy like the common bread.

And there is a familiar nursery rhyme that borrows some of these words:

Hot cross buns, hot cross buns,
If you have no daughters, give them to your sons.

Although buns may be plain or sweet, filled with currants and nuts or not, with or without icing, they do tend to resemble rounded knobs in shape. Therefore the word *bun* has been transferred to a number of other things shaped in roughly this way. Hair coiled in a rounded knot at the nape or top of the head is called a *bun;* the human buttocks are called *buns* (this term is always in the plural); and a pregnant woman is said *to have a bun in the oven.*

Finally, *to have a bun on* has meant, since about 1900, to be intoxicated, but the relationship of this usage to edible buns is unknown (and may not exist).

Muffins

Oh, do you know the muffin man,
the muffin man, the muffin man,
Do you know the muffin man
That lives in Drury Lane?
  —Nursery song

Curiously, Englanders are unfamiliar with the *English muffin,* which they would probably call a *crumpet.* Both terms refer to a small, soft, round yeast cake that is usually toasted and buttered before being served. In England a muffin is a light, flat, round, spongy cake, which in the olden days used to be sold by a street vendor (the muffin man in the song above), much as ice cream was sold on American streets.

In English slang, a *crumpet* is a head, and *barmy on the crumpet* means crazy in the head, whereas a *nice bit of crumpet* means a beautiful woman (in American slang, a *dish*).

Actually, the English muffin differs in important ways from other kinds of *muffin.* It is relatively flat and made with yeast.

The American muffin, in contrast, is cup-shaped, and indeed is baked in a pan containing a series of cuplike indentations (and called a *muffin pan*). Further, it is leavened with baking soda or baking powder and is not eaten toasted.

One common characteristic of both crumpets and muffins of any kind is that they are usually served at breakfast and/or tea-time. In America the latter gave rise to the name *muffin stand* for a small, multitiered stand used to hold cakes, muffins, and a tea service.

England's flat sort of muffin gave rise to other linguistic transfers: *muffin cap* for a flat cap worn by schoolboys; *muffin-face* for a blank, expressionless face; and *muffin-head* for a blockhead or dunce. None of these crossed the Atlantic.

The Toast of the Town

> For about fifteen minutes Doug Flutie was the toast of New York—not just the toast but the challah and the pita and the croissants, too.
>> —George Vecsey, *New York Times*
>> (Sept. 28, 1986), on the quarterback's being
>> signed to play for the New Jersey Generals

Toast is a slice of bread that has been made brown and more or less crisp by exposure to heat. This meaning of toast has been around since at least the fourteenth century. It accounts for the simile *warm as toast,* which remains current, as well as the figurative *to toast,* as in "toast one's feet by the fire," meaning simply to warm them.

How, then, did we get *drinking a toast* to someone, or becoming *the toast of the town*? The answer lies in the old British practice of placing a piece of spiced toast in a glass of sherry or other liquor. The *OED* quotes a cookbook of c. 1430 recommending the spices to be used (sugar, salt, pepper, and saffron), and Shakespeare's huge drinker, Falstaff, said, "Go, fetch me a quart of Sacke, put a tost in 't" (*The Merry Wives of Windsor,* 3:5).

Over the next two centuries the word *toast* was transferred first to the person in whose honor a drink is dedicated, and then to a good wish or compliment offered with the drink (also described as drinking to someone's "health"). At first this person was usually a lady, and in fact the magazine *Tatler* in 1702 described a particular incident said to be responsible for this transference. Supposedly during the reign of Charles I (1625–49) a beautiful woman appeared in the waters at Bath, a famous spa, and a gentleman in the crowd admiring her filled a glass with water in which she stood and drank her health. Although the gentleman said he did not like the taste, he would have the toast, meaning the lady, and that usage persisted until sometime in the eighteenth century, when *toast* began to signify the pledge itself. But the earlier usage survives in *toast of the town* for a person, often a performer, who is celebrated on some occasion or honored in some way.

In Britain, to have someone *on toast* means to have him or her at one's mercy, and to be *had on toast* means to be swindled. Neither slang term is heard much in America. For milk toast, see MILK.

As for the challah, pita, and croissants in the quotation above, they are specialty breads, respectively Jewish, Middle Eastern, and French in origin, but their names have not been transferred or used figuratively.

Crumbs and Crusts

He that keeps nor crust nor crumb,
Weary of all, shall want some.
> —William Shakespeare, *King Lear,* 1:4

The word *crumb* has meant a small particle of bread since the tenth century and has been used figuratively to denote a tiny bit of anything at all since the fourteenth century. It also once denoted the soft, inner part of bread, as opposed to the crisp outer part, or *crust.* This is what Shakespeare was alluding to in the quotation above, an alliterative way of saying that he who saves nothing will be sorry later.

Crumbs from the rich man's table appears in the Bible (Luke 16:21), where the beggar Lazarus hopes to be so fed. It has come to mean any slight consideration or small act of charity from the rich to the poor. From this, too, comes to *throw someone a crumb,* meaning to give the smallest amount that will placate someone.

You got a lot of crust, Turtle!
> —Neal Sternecky, *Pogo* comic strip,
> *Boston Globe,* Nov. 21, 1991

The bread crust, too, is used figuratively to mean something of slight value, because it is hard and dry. "For a *crust of bread* he can be hired either to keep silence or to speak," wrote Marcus Cato about 175 B.C., referring to the little it would take to bribe Marcus Caelius. The hardness of the crust also gave rise to the word's figurative use as an outer shell that is difficult to penetrate. This sense is further extended in the slang usage, *to have a lot of crust,* meaning to have impudence or effrontery, which dates from about 1900.

The pastry shell of pies also is called a *crust,* or *piecrust.* From it we have the *piecrust table,* a table with a round top that has an intricately carved edge, resembling the decoration of a piecrust. Both term and style originated in America about 1900.

It is probably also from piecrusts that we have the expression *upper crust* for the élite, the highest social class. Several authorities believe the term came from the ancient practice of slicing the top crust from a loaf of bread and presenting it to the king. However, this origin seems unlikely in view of the fact that in the olden days bread was simply torn into hunks rather than being neatly sliced. Further, the earliest reference to upper crust appeared in *The Clockmaker* (1835) by Thomas C. Haliburton (Sam Slick), "It was none of your skim-milk parties, but superfine uppercrust." The argument for its reference to pie rather than bread is that the upper crust of pie tends to be nicely browned and crisp, hence constituting the choicest part. The term was being used figuratively by others from about 1850 on.

Dough

BAGEL FIRM WANTS DOUGH—
SAYS JAMAICA PLAIN ARTS CENTER
OWES BACK RENT
                    —Headline, *Boston Globe,* Nov. 14, 1991

The word *dough* for a mixture of flour, water, and, sometimes, other ingredients has been around for at least a thousand years. Its slang use for money is American in origin and, largely, usage, and it dates from the mid-nineteenth century, but to date no one has advanced an explanation for this transfer.

That is not the case for the *doughboy,* a nickname for U.S. infantrymen for whose origin a number of different theories have been proposed. The one most widely subscribed to is that the large brass buttons on the mid-nineteenth century infantry uniform resembled a pastry originally baked for sailors, and the name was transferred from pastry to button to soldier. The earliest appearances of the word in print are dated 1867.

About forty years earlier southerners used the term *doughface* for any northerner who supported slavery in the South. This term was reportedly invented by John Randolph of Roanoke, Virginia, and some believed he really meant *doeface* (a deer being timid), but doughface is what stuck and continued to be so used until the end of the Civil War.

Also see DOUGHNUT.

The Sandwich Generation

The word *sandwich,* for two slices of bread filled with meat, cheese, or some other filling, supposedly was invented by John Montagu, Fourth Earl of Sandwich (1718–92), because he ordered meat between slices of bread, which he consumed during twenty-four-hour gambling bouts without interrupting play.

The term was soon transferred, serving as both noun and verb for layers resembling a sandwich or creating a sandwich (as in *to sandwich an evening meeting between the day-long seminars).* It was Dickens who invented the term *sandwich man* for the man carrying two connected posters or signboards (called a *sandwich board),* one hanging in front and the other behind. He had it in his *Sketches by "Boz"* (1836–39): "So, he stopped the unstamped advertisement—an animated sandwich, composed of a boy between two boards." A century and a half later Americans invented the term *sandwich generation,* for middle-aged persons charged with the responsibility of caring for and supporting both their children and their aged parents.

The word *sandwich* has acquired several other slang uses. In football and some other sports it means to trap an offensive player between two defenders. In real estate it refers to a rental agreement among three parties—landlord, tenant, and sub-letter of the property (also called a *sandwich lease*). And finally, alluding to sandwiches as the quintessential picnic food, *a few sandwiches short of a picnic* is said of a person who is considered not quite right in the head, a slangy synonym for having a few screws loose.

ELEVEN

Sweets to the Sweet

Sweets to the sweet have made much business for dentists.
—Anon., *Meditations on Wall Street* (1940)

Writers of dictionaries seem to have a hard time defining the adjective "sweet," other than it is pleasing to the taste, is characteristic of sugar and honey, and is a flavor quite distinct from "bitter," "sour," and "salty." However, in both ancient and modern times, the word for "sweet" has been related to things pleasant—as with the Latin *suavis* (sweet) and *suadere* (to make pleasant)—and the later extensions to "beloved," as in the famous line from *Hamlet,* "Sweets to the sweet" (uttered by the Queen scattering flowers at Ophelia's burial, 5:1).

Consequently *sweet talk* came to mean flattery; *sweetheart* became a synonym of lover (and, by extension, something excellent, such as a *sweetheart contract,* which favors union officials and management at the expense of the workers); and in the twentieth century the verb *to sweeten,* literally to make sweet or add a sweet substance such as honey or sugar, also came to mean enhancing the terms or value of a financial deal. And a *sweet tooth* has meant a love or craving for sweet-flavored foods since the fourteenth century, long before anyone associated sweets with tooth decay or knew how to repair damaged teeth.

Britons call both candy and such foods as cake or tarts *a sweet*. The latter often constitute the dessert course of a meal, which in Britain is also called *the sweet* or *pudding* (it may be followed by a salty dish such as cheese, called *a savory*).

Honey produced by wild bees was probably the first sweetening agent known, and the word has been used as a term of endearment since the fourteenth century. By the mid-sixteenth century we had *honeymoon,* for the first month of marriage, considered a time of peak pleasure and affection.

Sweetness can also be overdone, too cloying for comfort. This is the case with *syrupy,* derived from *syrup,* a general name for any thick, sweet flavoring liquid; a *syrupy greeting card,* for example, is one expressing mawkish sentiment. The same is true of *honeyed* words, meaning too flattering to be true. Although *sweetness and light* were first paired as two noble qualities c. A.D. 39 in a commentary on the Old Testament Book of Exodus, Jonathan Swift gave the term a satiric bent: "Instead of dirt and poison, we have rather chosen to fill our lives with honey and wax, thus furnishing mankind with the two noblest of things, which are sweetness and light" *(The Battle of the Books,* 1697).

Sugar

Sugar itself, in the form of sugar cane, was brought to the Western world only in the tenth century by Crusaders (it was cultivated earlier by the Chinese, who may have been the first to find a way of extracting the cane juice and using it for sweetening). The earliest use of sweets in Europe was to conceal the taste of bitter medicines. This practice survives in the *sugarcoated pill,* literally a medication coated with candy to improve its taste and figuratively any kind of cover-up to make something distasteful seem more palatable. The word *sugar* is also a term for endearment, as well as slang for money, a bribe, or drugs. A *sugar daddy* is an older man of wealth who spends it freely on a much younger woman for her companionship and, usually, sexual favors; the expression dates from about 1915, but the practice is, of course, much older.

Like Taking Candy from a Baby

Candy is dandy
But liquor is quicker.
—Ogden Nash, *Reflections on Ice-Breaking* (1931)

Nash's famous lines did not foresee the use of *nose candy,* as cocaine began to be called in America at just about the time he penned them *(candy* still serves as a slang term for various illegal drugs). Sniffing cocaine probably produces an even faster "high" than consuming alcohol, and the slang term transfers the sweetness and desirability of a confection to that of an addictive drug. Sugar is also, of course, a legitimate source of quick energy, and consequently candy bars are often included in hikers' backpacks, soldiers' field rations, and athletes' snacks.

Candy in America is a general name for many kinds of confection (usually called *sweets* in Britain). It comes from an Arabic word and originally referred to crystallized sugar, itself a confection.

A popular kind of candy in America is the red-and-white-striped peppermint cane, which gave rise to the term *candy-striped* for that particular design, dating from the late nineteenth century, and to *candy striper* for young volunteer hospital workers, so called for their brightly striped uniform since the 1960s.

Like taking candy from a baby has been, since the first half of the twentieth century, a common American simile for something ridiculously easy. And from the last decades of the century we have *ear candy,* for easy-on-the-ear music produced by a synthesizer. A related term is *bubble-gum music,* but that requires a bit of explanation. *Chewing gum* is not, strictly speaking, a food, but it is nearly always sweet. It is much older than one might think; Thornton's *American Glossary* says it is essentially the same as the "mouth glue" mentioned in Baret's *Alvearie* (1573–80), and John Bate gave a recipe for "mouth glew" in 1635, involving steeped isinglass. Whether or not this concoction crossed the Atlantic with early colonists is a matter of speculation. However, the term "chewing gum" is definitely American in origin, dating from the early nineteenth century, and involved chewing the gum of the spruce tree (spruce gum), a practice first mentioned in print in a Philadelphia newspaper of 1836. Several later citations refer to it as women's equivalent to chewing tobacco, which was a strictly male practice (at least in genteel circles). Only in the late nineteenth century was chewing gum as we know it today invented, that is, based on chicle, obtained from the latex of certain tropical American trees, mainly the sapodilla. In the 1930s gum manufacturers developed a new wrinkle, *bubble gum.* This type of gum can, when one uses the tongue and lips, be blown into large bubbles, and particularly appealed to youngsters. Consequently the term *bubblegummer* came to be used for young teenagers and preadolescents. At last we come to *bubble-gum music,* a term that began to be used in the late 1960s for the frothy rock music, with basic, repetitive phrasing and simple lyrics, favored by this age group.

The chicle that went into chewing gum gave rise to a trade name, *Chiclets,* for a brand of chewing gum made in small, rectangular, sugar-coated lozenges. In the early 1980s this name was transferred to a type of computer keyboard whose keys are smaller and closer together than those of a typewriter and lack the full movement of typewriter keys.

A popular kind of candy on both sides of the Atlantic is taffy, more often called *toffee* in Britain. This sticky, chewy confection gave rise, in Britain in the 1920s, to *toffee-nosed* as slang for stuck-up or pretentious. The term is occasionally heard in America as well.

Let Them Eat Cake

Most references to *cake*, generally defined as a sweet, breadlike food, are very positive, but for a time the word, along with *cakey*, referred to a foolish person. This usage, recorded in Grose's slang compendium of 1785, persisted in America until the mid-nineteenth century but has died out.

From approximately the same period comes the most famous utterance attributed to France's Queen Marie Antoinette. Allegedly, when told that the peasants were too poor to afford bread, she replied, "Then *let them eat cake*." Practically everything about this statement is questionable, including the translation. Jean-Jacques Rousseau, in his *Confessions* (c. 1768), attributed it to "a great princess," whom he did not name, who said, "Qu'ils mangent de la brioche," literally, "Let them eat brioche [a kind of coffeecake]." Marie Antoinette, Austrian by birth, did not arrive in France until 1770. Nevertheless, it is still widely quoted whenever invoking haughty disdain of the haves for the have-nots.

> *Dost thou think, because thou art virtuous, there shall be no more cakes and ale?*
> —William Shakespeare, *Twelfth Night*, 2:3

In ancient Egypt, offerings of cake and ale were presented to the spirits of the dead, but it is unlikely that Shakespeare knew of them. By his time *cakes and ale* meant the good things in this life, a meaning still current, although the expression is more common in Britain than in America. W. Somerset Maugham used it as the title of an early novel concerning his hero's rather wild youth, which helped the term to persist.

Taking the cake once meant literally winning the prize of a cake, which was awarded to the winners of the *cakewalk.* The practice of awarding such prizes was actually very old. According to the Greek playwright Aristophanes, the man who kept awake best for a night watch or a drinking party was awarded a cake of roasted wheat and honey (*The Knights,* 424 B.C.). Our current term, however, dates from the nineteenth-century American contest for blacks, in which couples walked arm in arm around a room and the cake was given to the most graceful walkers. By the 1880s *to take the cake* was being transferred to excelling at anything or winning any prize, and in the early twentieth century the name *cakewalk* was transferred to a strutting-step jazz dance, as well as the music for such dances.

To have one's cake and eat it, too has been a metaphor for having things both ways since the sixteenth century or earlier. It appeared in John Heywood's 1546 proverb collection and has been repeated ever since, particularly for money matters (spending and at the same time keeping money).

Why, exactly, *a piece of cake* became a metaphor for something very easy to do is a bit puzzling. The term apparently became popular in the Royal Air Force about 1938 and had become extremely widespread by the end of World War II. Eric Partridge claimed it was obsolete in Britain by the early 1970s, but it remains current in the United States.

If cake is a good thing, icing or frosting—that is, adding a

sweet, creamy filling or coating to it—is obviously an improvement. (Both names come from their resemblance to actual frost or ice, which of course applies only when they are white in color. Depending on the flavorings and food colors used, they can in theory be just about any color.) From this we have the metaphoric *frosting/icing on the cake,* said of anything that further improves an already desirable thing, situation, etc. (The word *frosting* also has been transferred to a technique of highlighting the hair by bleaching individual strands, but this usage alludes to its resemblance to hoarfrost, or particles of ice.)

> *Pat-a-cake, pat-a-cake, baker's man,*
> *Bake me a cake as fast as you can;*
> *Pat it and prick it, and mark it with B,*
> *Put it in the oven for baby and me.*
> —Nursery rhyme

Literally patting a frosted cake might be a bit messy, but the children's game of *pat-a-cake* (or *patty cake*) never really involved that. It is simply a clapping game for two that has delighted the very young since 1698 (or perhaps much longer, but that is when the above-quoted nursery rhyme, which is chanted while clapping, was first published, in Tom D'Urfey's *The Campaigners*).

Particular kinds of cake also have been transferred linguistically. The name of the traditional *wedding cake,* an elaborately decorated, multitiered affair, has been transferred to over-elaborate works of architecture and interior decoration, usually as a criticism of excess.

Cheesecake, a delicious, fluffy, light-colored, and very fattening concoction of butter, cream cheese, sugar and flour, began to be transferred in the 1930s to pictures of attractive women displaying their physical charms. At first confined to their photographs, the term was later extended to the women themselves. (John Ciardi believed it was first coined about 1912 by *New York Journal* photographer James Kane, but the first printed citations date from the 1930s.) Exactly why cheesecake is a matter of speculation; perhaps the fluffy consistency and light color of the cake seemed similar to the lacy lingerie displayed in such pictures. Or perhaps it was a version of *cupcake,* also a term of endearment for an attractive woman.

Bowlers use *cheesecake* to signify a lane in which it is easy to make strikes and high scores (it is also called *pie alley,* probably alluding to *easy as pie;* see PIE below).

A *jelly roll* is a rectangular sponge cake that is spread with fruit jelly or jam and rolled up. In late nineteenth-century America the word also signified vulgar slang for sexual intercourse and for the vagina. In this guise it turned up in numerous blues lyrics (which often used such seemingly innocent words with a double meaning) as well as in the preferred nickname of Ferdinand *"Jelly Roll" Morton* (1885?–1941), self-proclaimed inventor of jazz and one of its outstanding and most colorful early practitioners.

Gingerbread, a spicy cake made with molasses and ginger,

has been so called since the fifteenth century. It formerly was made into various shapes—persons, animals, alphabet letters, etc.—and often decorated with gilt. In Britain it was widely sold at street fairs, and there the word *gingerbread* came to signify something tawdry, showy but without real value. It also gave rise to the saying *take the gilt off the gingerbread*, meaning to destroy the illusion or take away the attraction. The popular fairy tale of Hansel and Gretel, in which the wicked witch lived in a gingerbread house, may have given added currency to the construction of such houses, stuck together with thick frosting and ornamented with more frosting and candy. It may be from these that we have the term *gingerbread style of architecture*, for gaudily overornamented buildings, although this usage, too, may be derived from the earlier use of gingerbread for tawdry. In any event, *gingerbread* still is used for superfluous and showy architectural decoration, which was particularly popular during the late Victorian era.

Finally, for *sell like hot cakes* see under PANCAKES.

Chocolate

Despite the widespread popularity of chocolate in the form of candy, cake, and other delectable kinds of junk food, the word, known in English since about 1600, has not been transferred a great deal. Chocolate was first brought to Europe from Central America in the sixteenth century and was used mainly to make hot chocolate, or cocoa. As such it was served in London coffee houses, one of which actually had the name Cocoa Tree. The commercial production of chocolate candy dates only from the nineteenth century. It often was sold in elaborately decorated boxes, giving rise to the term *chocolate box* for excessively ornamented and sentimental designs and decorations.

Chocolate candies also were made in elaborate forms. One such kind was the *chocolate soldier,* a term then extended, about 1900, to soldiers who did not fight (were assigned to noncombatant jobs). The term was still current during World War II; in Australia it was shortened to *Chocos,* applied mainly to conscripts and militiamen.

In the second half of the twentieth century persons exceedingly fond of chocolate began to describe themselves as *chocoholics,* akin to those addicted to alcohol (alcoholics).

Finally, gynecologists refer to the cysts of endometriosis, which are filled with old (brown) blood, as *chocolate cysts.*

An extremely popular form of chocolate candy is *fudge,* a name originating in mid-nineteenth-century America. Although in eighteenth-century Britain this word also came to be used as an expletive, a synonym of nonsense or rubbish, as well as signifying defeat, the ultimate origin of this usage is obscure and probably has nothing to do with chocolate. (The verb form *to fudge* also has nothing to do with the confection.)

Smart Cookies

The word *cookie* most probably comes from the Dutch *koekje,* for "little cake," and was acquired from the New Amsterdam settlers during their fifty years of conflict with the English, although it also surfaced in Scotland about 1730. The British call cookies "sweet biscuits," and they are nearly as popular as a snack and dessert as they are in America.

Old as it is, the word *cookie* only began to be transferred to an attractive young woman by the twentieth century, as well as being used as an informal term of address, equivalent to "sweetheart" or "dear." At the same time, to be a *smart cookie* signifies shrewdness—Noël Coward wittily translated it into

"British" as "clever biscuit"—whereas a *tough cookie* is an intractable individual.

> *At the very least we can make Ronnie sweat. Always a good*
> *idea to make a clown with his hands in the cookie jar sweat.*
> —Barbara Probst Solomon,
> *Smart Hearts in the City* (1992)

To have one's *hand in the cookie jar* indicates one is helping oneself to something without being entitled to it—usually money or some other form of emolument. To be a *cookie pusher,* on the other hand, indicates one who has quite low government rank and is relegated to passing cookies and other refreshments at official receptions. Overindulgence in refreshments might lead one to *toss* or *spill one's cookies,* a euphemism for vomiting. All these terms date from the mid-twentieth century, as does *that's the way the cookie crumbles,* meaning that's fate, usually said when an outcome is less than ideal; it was particularly associated with the New York advertising world of the 1950s, which also came up with such metaphors as, "Run it up the flagpole and see if it will fly."

Cookie bakers will tell you that cookie dough may be rolled, dropped, or refrigerated and sliced. Rolled cookies are generally cut into special shapes such as circles or stars by using a *cookie cutter,* a metal or plastic form. In the second half of the twentieth century this term was sometimes transferred to other objects with exactly the same configuration—for example, "the cookie-cutter houses in this cheap development."

Toward the end of the twentieth century computer hacks transferred "cookie" in a number of novel ways. A *cookie* was an identifying mark given to someone who shared a computer program with others. A *magic cookie* was the pass allowing a user to move from one computer program or routine to another, and a *fortune cookie* a joke or saying shared on computer screens. The former is not a specific kind of cookie, but the latter alludes to the staple dessert of American Chinese restaurants, a thin, folded wafer surrounding a slip of paper bearing a prediction or maxim.

Oreo is the trade name of a cookie consisting of two chocolate wafers filled with white vanilla cream. In the 1960s the name began to be used as disparaging slang for a black person who adopts the behavior and attitudes of a middle-class white person, and denies or ignores his or her black heritage. The usage alludes to the cookie in that it describes someone who is black on the outside and white inside.

Another cookie somewhat like the Oreo is the *Twinkie,* which consists of two layers of chocolate cake filled with white vanilla cream. Considered the ultimate junk food, rich in sugar and fat and lacking beneficial nutrients, it surfaced in the late twentieth century in an imaginative lawyer's defense plea. He invoked what someone called a *Twinkie defense,* contending that his client's judgment had been impaired by eating too many foods high in sugar.

Still newer is *Twinkie economics,* for economic policy that pleases the voters but does not address such problems as the budget deficit. This term probably was invented by Paul Tsongas, contender for the Democratic presidential nomination in 1991, who said that his party would have to stop serving up "Twinkie economics" in order to defeat incumbent President George Bush. In 1992 he repeated it during a primary debate, saying, "I oppose Twinkie economics . . . tastes great but [has] no nutritional value" (Cincinnati CNN-TV news, March 1, 1992; cited in *American Speech,* 68.2, 1993).

> *Buy me some peanuts and crackerjack,*
> *I don't care if I never get back. . . .*
> >   —Jack Norworth, "Take Me
> >   Out to the Ball Game" (1908)

These lines from the unofficial anthem of America's national game indicate that fans have been munching on peanuts and crackerjack for a very long time indeed. Capitalized, *Cracker Jack* was, and still is, the trade name for a confection of caramel-coated popcorn and peanuts. In lower case, *crackerjack* has been used since about 1875 to describe a person or thing of marked excellence. The ultimate origin of the word is not known, but it is probably safe to speculate that it combined "crack," meaning excellent (as in "crack shot") and "jack," for any man (as in "every man jack"). Capitalizing on this usage both literally and figuratively, an American manufacturer, F. W. Rueckheims and Brother, adopted it for their confection.

Crackers

Cracker Jack has nothing to do with the *cracker,* a snack food known as a "biscuit" in Britain. In America crackers are not usually sweet, so strictly speaking they do not belong in this chapter. There are exceptions, however. *Animal crackers,* small cookies in the shape of animals, have been around since the late nineteenth century. They lent their name to the Marx Brothers' second movie *(Animal Crackers,* 1930), which has little to do with the cookie but a good deal to do with the British slang meaning of *crackers,* that is, eccentric or slightly insane.

In late eighteenth-century America *cracker* had two meanings. One was the current one of biscuit; an advertisement in the *Newport Mercury* of Feb. 7, 1774, said, "William Grinnell has to sell Ship-Bread, Crackers in barrels and kegs, etc." Crackers were, until about 1900, shipped in barrels, whence we have both the literal and the figurative senses of *cracker barrel.* Country grocery stores sold crackers straight from the barrel, which provided a center of activity for customers who came to the store for small talk and gossip as well as for purchases. By about 1875 *cracker-barrel* was used to describe country people and their homespun philosophy and directness.

The second meaning of *cracker,* also dating from the late eighteenth century, was an unflattering name for a poor southern white. Thornton *(An American Glossary)* believed it alluded to their habit of cracking whips with a soft piece of dry buckskin (called a "cracker") at the end, whereas Mathews *(A Dictionary of Americanisms)* believed it came from an earlier dialect use of cracker for a braggart or boaster and cites a 1766 letter from Gavin Cochrane to the Earl of Dartmouth. Whichever is true, the term was used particularly for people from Georgia, which thus acquired the nickname *Cracker State,* and the usage today is considered both disparaging and offensive, akin to the related "redneck."

Finally, the British say "cracker" when Americans would say "firecracker," which, of course, has nothing to do with anything edible.

Cream Puffs and Doughnuts

The cream puff is a hollow pastry made of what the French call *pâté à chou,* or puff pastry, and filled with custard or whipped cream. Its light and airy character (despite its high caloric content) made the name be transferred to a weak, ineffectual person or thing. For example, in tennis a weak second serve is sometimes called a *cream puff.* At the same time, in the used-car industry, cream puff denotes an automobile in exceptionally good condition.

The earliest printed reference to the *doughnut* appears in Washington Irving's *History of New York* (1809): "An enormous dish of balls of sweetened dough, fried in hog's fat, and called *dough nuts* or *oly koeks."* The latter name is Dutch, and indeed, this fried pastry is well known in Holland, Austria, and other European countries. In Austria, jelly-filled doughnuts, called *Krapfen,* are traditional New Year's Eve fare.

Exactly when American bakers began to make ring-shaped doughnuts (or *donuts)* is not certain, but it is allusions to these that have given rise to numerous linguistic transfers. In automotive slang, *donuts* are automobile tires, and to *do donuts,* meaning to drive in tight circles, is a popular sport among young car thieves. A *doughnut cushion,* a thick, inflatable ring, makes sitting much more comfortable following injury or surgery involving the posterior, enabling it to avoid direct contact with the chair. In radio broadcasting, a *donut* is slang for a gap in a radio commercial that allows for the insertion of a local announcement. In Great Britain, *doughnutting* is a practice in which members of Parliament form a ring around a fellow member who is speaking during a televised session, to make home viewers think that the House is very crowded when in fact it may be half empty. The term dates from 1989, when TV cameras were first allowed into the House of Commons.

In nineteenth-century Britain such sayings as "all Lombard

Street to a ninepence" signified heavy odds (Lombard Street in London being occupied by most major banks). Around the turn of the twentieth century Americans had a similar expression with the same meaning, *to lay dollars to doughnuts,* first recorded in a Utica (New York) newspaper in 1904, and *dollars to doughnuts* alone came to indicate a virtual certainty. Although it is heard less often today, its survival was probably linked more to alliteration than meaning.

Finally, Tom Wolfe, in his novel *The Bonfire of the Vanities* (1987), used the term *electric doughnut* for a person known only through telephone calls; the allusion here is to the rounded mouthpiece on old-time telephones. However, this usage is far from widespread and may turn out to be short-lived.

A close relative of the doughnut is the *fritter,* which is also made of deep-fried dough and often contains fruit, corn, clams, or some other ingredient. The verb *to fritter* means to waste or squander, but in this instance the identical words have nothing to do with one another. The edible fritter's name comes from the Latin for "to fry," whereas the verb comes from the old English *fitter,* or fit, for a small part.

> *Diddle diddle dumpling, my son John,*
> *Went to bed with his britches on.*
> —Nursery rhyme

Unlike doughnuts, which can be round, straight or twisted oblong (crullers), or rings, *dumplings* are always round. The steamed and seasoned variety are often served in stews or soups, whereas the baked or boiled variety enclose apples or some other fruit and are served for dessert. As long ago as the seventeenth century their roundness led the word to be transferred to a short, plump person. Grose's dictionary of colloquialisms held that this usage originated as a jeering term for a Norfolk man, dumplings being a favorite food in that county.

In dialect, *dumpling* also meant a fool or blockhead, but this usage is no longer current, at least not in America.

Another dessert of British provenance is *flummery,* which began life in Wales as a cereal rather than a sweet. Called *llymru* in Gaelic, it was made by soaking oatmeal in water for several days. When the water had taken up enough starch, the oats were removed and the water boiled into a gelatinous stew. The English took the name in the seventeenth century and anglicized it to flummery, which by the eighteenth century began to refer to sweet, starchy puddings (as it still does) and also to its still current figurative meaning, empty flattery or foolish talk, or nonsense. *New York Times* columnist Anthony Lewis used "flummery" to describe what Senator Arlen Specter said during the Senate Judiciary Committee hearings on Clarence Thomas's nomination to the U.S. Supreme Court (October 1991).

Flavor of the Month

Ice cream, the frozen food made from milk or cream, sugar, and flavorings, dates back to the mid-eighteenth century. Water ices, made from frozen juice and other clear beverages, antedate it by at least half a century, but their name was not transferred. At first ice cream was mainly a home-made or restaurant dessert, but by the turn of the twentieth century numerous American cities and towns had an *ice cream parlor,* which sold ice cream in the form of sodas and sundaes as well as plain. The traditional décor of such establishments gave rise to the name *ice cream parlor chair,* for a side chair made of heavy wire and with a round wooden seat.

The most popular flavor of ice cream in America is vanilla, which is cream-colored or nearly white. From it came the name *ice cream pants* for men's summer pants of a creamy white, usually worn with a dark-blue blazer. Of similar provenance is the *ice cream suit,* a light-colored lightweight summer suit for men. Both terms date from the late nineteenth century but are heard less often nowadays.

In the twentieth century American purveyors of ice cream faced stiff competition and therefore tried to attract customers in various ways. One such ploy was featuring a different flavor of ice cream each month, and urging people to try this *flavor of the month,* sometimes lowering the price to convince them. By about 1980 this term had been transferred to describe anything that was temporarily popular or in fashion. For example, a 1981 article in *The Economist* said actor Peter Sellers reportedly "experimented with faiths and fortunetellers on a flavor-of-the-month basis" (cited by Jeffrey McQuayle, *New York Times,* Aug. 30, 1992).

In Britain, *ice creamer* is derogatory slang for an Italian, because in the early twentieth century many Italian immigrants worked as ice cream vendors.

Flat as a Pancake

Beat all your feathers as flat as pancakes.
—Thomas Middleton, *The Roaring Girl,* 2:1 (1611)

Pancake or griddle cake, hot cake or flapjack, flannel cake or batter cake, johnnycake or hoecake—all these names signify a thin, flat cake of batter that is fried on both sides on a griddle or in a frying pan. Their flatness made them the object of a simile we still use—*flat as a pancake*—from the late sixteenth century on. Pancakes were a traditional food for Shrove Tuesday, immediately preceding Lent, which thus was also called

Pancake Tuesday. It was a day of festivities sounded off by ring-ing the *Pancake Bell,* a signal for people to stop work and go home to make pancakes. In some English towns and villages a Pancake Day race is still held every year.

A number of terms allude to pancakes. *Pancake ice,* so called since the early nineteenth century, is newly formed ice that is quite flat and thin and therefore does not impede navigation. In twentieth-century America *Pan-Cake* became the trade name of a cosmetic consisting of a flat cake of compressed powder, which is applied with a moist sponge. The verb *to pancake* means to flatten; in aeronautics slang it means to drop flat to the ground after leveling off the aircraft a few feet above it. The latter maneuver is also called a *pancake landing.* And in the days of long-playing records, a disc jockey was sometimes called a *pancake handler,* a locution dying out with newer technology.

Hot cakes has been an American name for pancakes since the late seventeenth century, and they have long been a popular item at church fairs and similar gatherings featuring food stands. Indeed, they often are sold as quickly as they can be made, whence the expression *to sell like hot cakes,* for any great commercial success.

A variant on the pancake is the *waffle,* made from a similar batter but baked in a gridlike pattern between two patterned irons. The word comes from the Dutch *wafel,* as does *waffle iron,* a direct translation of the Dutch *wafelijzer.* From it we have the *wafflestomper,* a hiking boot with ridged soles, and the *waffle weave* of some textiles, roughly resembling a waffle pat-tern. John Ciardi believed the verb *to waffle,* meaning to speak or write equivocally, or to vacillate, also comes from the edible waffle (the up-and-down pattern somehow being transferred to the back-and-forth of double-talk), but the *OED* and other lex-icons point to different origins, among them the Scottish dia-lect word, *waffle,* meaning to flutter or wave.

Easy as Pie

Pie, n[oun]. An advance agent of the reaper whose name is Indigestion.
—Ambrose Bierce, *The Devil's Dictionary* (1881–1906)

In England the word *pie* usually means baked meat or fish inside a pastry crust. In the sixteenth century it also began to be used for fruits in a pastry crust, and it is this meaning that crossed the Atlantic and persists in America, where a pie is nearly always a pastry filled with apples or some other fruit (see also APPLE-PIE ORDER and APPLE-PIE BED in the chapter on fruit; PIECRUST TABLE in the chapter on bread and dough; and TART later in this chapter).

Ambrose Bierce's comment notwithstanding, in late nineteenth-century America the word *pie* signified a prize or a treat, particularly a division of spoils. From this period we also have *slice of the pie,* for a portion of the profits or spoils, an expression still current, as well as two other phrases that are probably obsolete: *pie counter,* a figurative sales counter where spoils may be obtained, and *pie hunter* for a person on the lookout for plunder.

A number of expressions allude to the traditional round shape of pies. The *pie chart,* a term used since about 1920, is a graphic representation of quantities consisting of a circle divided into sectors, in effect resembling slices of pie. A person described as *pie-faced* has a round, flat face, bearing a blank expression that implies stupidity. This term dates from about 1910. From roughly the same time comes the slang word *pie-eyed* for intoxicated, so much so that it affects one's vision.

Something *easy as pie* is ridiculously simple. Presumably this expression, dating from the early 1900s, refers to consuming something delicious rather than making a pie, which requires a degree of skill. The same is meant by *nice as pie,* meaning well behaved and otherwise pleasant, but no longer heard very often, and *sweetie pie,* a term of endearment. Still another favorable allusion to pie is *pie in the sky,* which has meant a promised good life that never arrives ever since it appeared in 1911 in the rallying song of the International Workers of the World, or Wobblies:

> *You will eat, bye and bye, in the glorious land above the*
> *sky!*
> *Work and pray, live on hay, you'll get pie in the sky when*
> *you die.*

In contrast, to *eat humble pie* means to, in effect, eat one's words, to acknowledge an error and abase oneself. The expression alludes to the meat pies of Britain; it is a corruption or pun on "umble-pie," umbles being a dialect word for the internal organs of a deer (heart, liver, entrails), which were given to servants and beaters while the lord and his guests feasted on the choice venison.

> *The Queen of Hearts, she made some tarts*
> *All on a summer's day;*
> *The Knave of Hearts, he stole the tarts,*
> *And took them clean away.*
> —Nursery rhyme, *European Magazine,* April 1782

In Britain today, America's fruit pie is usually called a *tart* but has no top crust (is open-faced). In mid-nineteenth century Britain this word was also lower-class affectionate slang for a young woman, a usage Ebenezer Brewer thought might come from a shortening of "sweetheart" but which other lexicographers regard more as a transfer from a delicious dessert to an attractive woman. A few decades later, however, the word began to signify a prostitute, a meaning that persists. This usage was further embellished, according to Tom Wolfe's 1987 novel, *The Bonfire of the Vanities,* into *lemon tart:* "These women in their twenties or early thirties, mostly blondes (the Lemon in the Tarts), who were the second, third, and fourth wives or live-in girlfriends of men over forty or fifty or sixty (or seventy)" (cited by William Safire, *New York Times,* Aug. 30, 1992).

Proof of the Pudding

Until about 1800, the word *pudding* nearly always signified a sausage of some kind—that is, a meat-filled casing. In America this usage survives primarily in *black pudding* or blood sausage, a dark sausage with a high blood content. In Britain the word "pudding" alone often signifies the dessert course of a meal, whether or not it consists of the thick, soft, sweet mixture so called by Americans.

A version that falls into neither category is *hasty pudding,* a favorite supper dish in colonial New England. Today more often called *cornmeal mush,* it consists of a mixture of cornmeal and boiling water that is steamed and served hot with molasses or milk, or sugar and butter. It was so called because it could be cooked and served in a relatively short time. It figures in the song *Yankee Doodle* (c. 1765):

> *And there we saw the men and boys*
> *As thick as hasty pudding.*

Its name is immortalized in Harvard University's *Hasty Pudding Club,* an élite social club known for its theatrical productions.

Whichever kind of pudding is meant, meat or sweet, *the proof of the pudding is in the eating,* meaning that performance rather than looks is the critical test, an adage that has been repeated ever since William Camden first wrote it down in 1605 (in *Remains Concerning Britain).* Another old expression is *pudding time,* meaning dinnertime (because meat pudding was a traditional first dish); it was then extended to mean the critical or opportune moment.

Finally, we have Mark Twain's renowned *Pudd'nhead Wilson* (1893), about Mr. David Wilson, a young attorney newly arrived in town. One day a yelping, snarling dog caused him to say that he wished he owned half of that dog because he then would kill his half. This statement aroused considerable talk among the townspeople, one of whom, identified only as No. 6, said, "Perfect jackass—yes, and it ain't going too far to say he is a pudd'nhead." And within a week, Twain continues, Wilson had lost his first name, and Pudd'nhead took its place. The reference here undoubtedly is to the soft consistency of puddings, transferred to being somewhat soft in the head, or foolish.

(For PLUM PUDDING, see the chapter on fruits.)

Closely related to pudding is *junket,* a sweet custard made of milk curded with rennet. Today the word also signifies a trip, a usage derived over the centuries. The word "junket" originally (fourteenth century) meant a rush basket for carrying various foods, and in the fifteenth century was transferred to a creamy cheese mixture that was made in such baskets. In the sixteenth century, however, the word was further extended to mean a feast or a banquet accompanied by merrymaking, and it is probably this usage that helped junket become, in late nineteenth-century America, any pleasurable outing in which eating and drinking played a part. And finally this meaning in turn was extended to a politician's trip made at government expense. From the last we also have *junketeer,* in noun form describing someone who frequently goes on junkets and in verb form (*to junketeer*) describing the process, as in, "For a time congressmen were regularly junketeering to Vietnam to observe matters at first hand."

Still another kind of pudding is *mousse,* whose name is French for "froth." It usually consists of egg yolks, whipped cream, stiffly beaten egg whites, sometimes gelatin, and flavoring ranging from melted chocolate (for a dessert mousse) to puréed fish, vegetables, or meats (for a main course). In the 1960s the consistency of mousse caused the name to be transferred to a foamy hairdressing preparation, used to keep hair in place, to give it more body, or to color it.

TWELVE

*Drink and
Be Merry*

Liquids are at least as vital for sustaining life as solid foods—some would argue even more so. We saw that *meat and drink,* meaning food and drink, signified life's essentials as well as a source of great enjoyment (see MEAT). The latter is emphasized in the expression *Eat, drink, and be merry,* which appeared in the Old Testament Book of Isaiah (22:13), dating from about 725 B.C. In this instance it is followed by *for tomorrow we shall die,* but later references, in Ecclesiastes, Luke, and nonbiblical texts, do not always include the warning that life is short and so should be enjoyed right now.

The gods of the ancient Greeks lived on more exalted food and drink. They ate *ambrosia* and drank *nectar,* which conferred immortality on them. Today "ambrosia" signifies any delicious flavor or fragrance, and "nectar" any delicious drink, which gave its name to the *nectarine.*

Liquids that we drink, other than plain water, are generally called *beverages,* and themselves consist mainly of water. Necessary as it is, a diet consisting solely of *bread and water* is considered harsh fare, such as might be given in punishment or penance. Water itself has given rise to the transferred *watered down,* for diluted, and the slangy *long drink of water,* for a tall, thin person. Susan Isaacs had it in her novel *Magic Hour* (1991): "One of them, a gangly kid my grandmother would have called a long drink of water, came into the tent."

Besides pure water, the principal beverages we consume are milk (discussed in the chapter on dairy products); juices expressed from fruits and vegetables (see ORANGE for an example referring to juice); alcoholic beverages such as ale and beer, rum, whiskey, mixed drinks, wine and champagne; caffeine-containing beverages such as coffee and tea; and so-called "soft" drinks, usually carbonated and devoid of alcohol. Virtually all of these have given us linguistic transfers, as have some of the containers used for liquid refreshment.

Ale and Beer

All beverages that are brewed, or boiled, from grains and then fermented are called *beer.* The term includes *ale,* a strong, fruity beer fermented at a warmer temperature, and *porter* and *stout,* dark ales with a roasted malt.

The principal grain used to make beer is malted barley, although wheat, corn, rye, millet, rice, and other vegetables and even fruits have been boiled to produce a beerlike beverage in the 6,000 or so years since the process of beermaking was discovered.

Beer is believed to be as old as agriculture. As soon as humans learned to harvest the products of the soil, they learned to fit them into their diet, and bread and beer were among the earliest processed foods. Brewing was a household art, like cooking and baking, until medieval times, when the brew houses of monasteries carried on the work.

Beer came to America with the *Mayflower,* whose journal reported, ". . . we could not now take time for further search or consideration; our victuals being much spent, especially our beer." Beer was considered by many to be a regular part of the daily diet, and many prominent early Americans were brewers. George Washington's recipe for beer is still preserved in his handwriting in the New York Public Library.

Britain has long been known as a nation of beer drinkers, justly famous for its alehouses and pubs. The words *ale* and *beer* originally were synonymous; today beer is a generic name for all malt liquors, whereas ale denotes the pale-colored varieties, for which the malt has not been roasted or burned. However, there are regional differences in terminology throughout the British Isles.

In Britain an *alewife* has been, since the fourteenth century, a woman who keeps an alehouse. In America, however, this word has meant, since the early seventeenth century, a herring-like fish, *Alosa pseudoherengus* to zoologists, which is found in great numbers along the Atlantic coast. An early reference to it occurs in *New Plymouth Laws* (1633): "That therefore the said herrings alewives or shadds comonly used in the setting of corne be appropriated." The origin of this name is not known for sure, but as the quotation indicates, the fish was a kind used in planting corn. A number of seeds would be set on a small mound of earth, with a fish stuck into the soil among them to act as a fertilizer. The early colonists learned this method from the native Americans. Some linguists believe the name also is an adaptation of an Indian word, but most think it came from an English dialect word for a fish, which in turn may have been derived from the alehouse keeper. The fish name, incidentally, survives in New England; a small stream in Cambridge, Massachusetts, called Alewife Brook, gave its name to the highway alongside it, Alewife Brook Parkway.

Another largely British expression is *small beer,* originally (sixteenth century) meaning weak beer and by the mid-nineteenth century turned into a colloquialism for insignificant or small-time.

Yet another, based on British custom, is *not all beer and skittles,* meaning not all fun and games. Skittles is a kind of bowling game that involves throwing wooden disks at pins; beer drinking is a similarly popular form of recreation. They began to be linguistically paired in the nineteenth century, most often in the expression "Life is not all beer and skittles." It crossed the Atlantic to America but is not heard much today.

In America, a potbelly or paunch has been called a *beer belly* since the early twentieth century. A newer bit of American slang reflecting another aftereffect of beer consumption is *beergoggles,* which according to Paul Dickson indicates perception (or vision) impaired by imbibing alcohol.

Another country known for its beer consumption is Germany. In the nineteenth century, German immigrants brought two of their native establishments to America, the *Biergarten,* translated into beer garden, and the *Bierhalle,* or beer hall. The first was simply an outdoor tavern, in effect a garden adjacent to an indoor tavern, where beer and other refreshments were consumed. It often featured musical entertainment as well, provided by so-called *lager-beer musicians.* Among the latter were the first successful all-women's orchestras, such as the Vienna Ladies Orchestra of the 1870s and their many imitators. The most famous of them was the Ladies Elite Orchestra, which performed at the Atlantic Garten, in lower Manhattan, for more than thirty-five years.

The beer hall was an indoor version of the same kind of establishment, serving beer and offering entertainment. Its name, too, was a translation from the German, but it achieved even greater notoriety in the 1920s through what has gone down in history as the *Beer Hall Putsch.* On November 12, 1923, in Munich's largest beer hall, the Bürgerbräukeller, Adolf Hitler and his Brown Shirts interrupted a speech by Gustav von Kahr, the state commissioner, and tried to take over the Bavarian state government. Hitler declared that he was supported by Germany's great World War I hero, Field Marshal Erich von Ludendorff. The attempt failed, however. Both Hitler and Ludendorff were arrested, and Hitler spent the next year in prison, where he wrote *Mein Kampf.* The word *Putsch,* incidentally, which means "insurrection" or "riot," became indelibly associated with this event.

Liquor's Quicker

Licker talks mighty loud when it gets loose fum de jug.
— Joel Chandler Harris,
Uncle Remus. Plantation Proverbs

Although the word *liquor* can mean any liquid substance, such as broth from cooked meats or vegetables, its most common usage is for alcoholic beverages that are distilled, such as rum or whiskey, as opposed to being fermented, such as wine or beer. All distilled spirits start with a fermented alcoholic solution of fruit or grain. Sometimes they are referred to as *hard liquor*. The word is also used as a verb, *to liquor* or *to liquor up*, meaning to imbibe quantities of such beverages.

A very old slang expression for liquor that remains current is *booze*, similarly used as both noun and verb (*to booze* or *booze it up* means to drink liquor, usually in quantity). The verb in particular has been around in various forms—*bouze, bouse, boowse*—since the fourteenth century. A modern linguistic offshoot is the *booze cruise*, any kind of boat trip where consuming liquor figures as an important element of entertainment.

The principal kinds of distilled spirits are whiskey, brandy, and rum, which are discussed below, and gin and vodka.

This calls the Church to deprecate our sin,
And hurls the thunder of the laws on gin.
— Alexander Pope, *Epilogue to the Satires*

Gin, made from alcohol and water, is usually flavored with juniper berries, whence its name (*genièvre* is French for "juniper"). Like most distilled spirits, gin is quite strong—its alcohol content ranges from forty to fifty percent—but it is colorless and does not have much flavor of its own. Consequently it often is mixed with more strongly flavored agents—lemon or lime (a gin rickey), quinine water (gin and tonic), vermouth (a fortified wine; see MARTINI under MIXED DRINKS, later in this chapter), and so on.

In mid-nineteenth-century America, a disreputable saloon was known as a *gin mill*. In Britain during the same period, a garishly ornate gin shop was called a *gin palace*. Numerous eminent lexicographers, including those of the estimable *OED*, believe that the name of the card game of *gin rummy* is derived from gin, but none presents any convincing evidence for this origin. The game, a version of rummy in which a player with ten or fewer points in unmatched cards can lay down his or her hand and end the game, originated in America about 1940.

Russians will consume marinated mushrooms and vodka, salted herring and vodka, smoked salmon and vodka, salami and vodka, caviar on brown bread and vodka, pickled cucumbers and vodka, cold tongue and vodka, red beet salad and vodka, scallions and vodka—anything and everything with vodka.

—Hedrick Smith, *The Russians* (1976)

Vodka, distilled chiefly from rye but also from potatoes, barley, or other materials, resembles gin in being colorless and virtually tasteless. Outside the former Soviet Union, it is, like gin, usually served in mixed drinks with fruit juice or some other, more highly flavored substance (vodka collins, vodka martini, etc.). But unlike gin, it is so closely identified with Russia that it is a virtual synonym for that country and its people. Thus the phrase *on the vodka circuit,* coined by *Newsweek* magazine in 1949, is instantly understood to mean a journey or round of activity involving something Russian.

Brandy

Brandy, n. A cordial composed of one part thunder-and-lightning, one part remorse, two parts bloody murder, one part death-hell-and-the-grave and four parts clarified Satan.
—Ambrose Bierce,
The Devil's Dictionary (1881–1906)

Brandy is distilled from wine, in turn made by fermenting grapes. A product labeled "brandy" is pure grape brandy. Indeed, the name *brandy* is a shortening of *brandywine* (still a common place name in America and site of a major British victory during the American Revolution, in 1777). Brandywine in turn is thought to come from Dutch words meaning "burned wine," that is, distilled wine. Brandy is very strong, which accounts for Bierce's above-quoted definition.

That Demon Rum

Rum is the bane of morals, and the parent of idleness.
—George Washington, letter to
Comte de Moustier, Dec. 15, 1788

Rum is distilled from the fermented juice of sugarcane, from fermented molasses, or from a mixture of these two. It is a New World product, brought to Europe and America from the West Indies. Its alcoholic content is very high, forty to fifty percent, making it one of the strongest liquors available. Probably for this reason it became a principal target for nineteenth-century supporters of the temperance movement, who labeled it "the Demon Rum."

In nineteenth-century America, *rum* also became a general name for all intoxicating liquors, giving rise to the related *rummy* for a drunkard or alcoholic, *rum-mill* for a tavern or liquor store, and *rum-running* for smuggling any kind of liquor (to evade the taxes on it). In Britain, on the other hand, the adjective *rum* began to be used in the late eighteenth century for anything odd or peculiar or problematic. A *rum situation,* therefore, is a difficult one, and a *rum fellow* is an odd or eccentric person. The connection between this usage and the liquor is unclear, but there probably is one.

Rum was a drink beloved by British sailors, so much so that drunkenness was a major shipboard problem. To improve matters on his ships, in 1740 Admiral Edward Vernon (?–1757) ordered that the daily rum ration allotted to his men be diluted with water. The sailors had nicknamed Vernon *Old Grog,* alluding to his habitual garb of a cloak made of *grogram,* a coarse fabric; its name came from the French *grosgrain* (in turn meaning "large grain"). The admiral's nickname was quickly transferred to the rum-and-water beverage, known to this day as *grog.* The latter also gave rise to the adjective *groggy,* originally meaning intoxicated but later applied to such manifestations of drunkenness or sleep deprivation as feeling shaky, wobbly on one's feet, or dazed. In nineteenth-century America a low saloon, usually unlicensed, was referred to as a *grog shop, grog mill,* or *groggery.*

Whiskey

Oh it's whiskey, whiskey, whiskey
That makes you feel so frisky
In the Corps, in the Corps. . . .
　　　　　　　　—Army drinking song, World War I

Whiskey includes rye, made from at least fifty-one per-cent rye grain; bourbon, made of fifty-one percent corn (the rest is usually barley, malted and unmalted); Canadian whis-key, generally distilled from a rye and barley mash; Scotch whiskey, blended from Highland (pure barley-malt mash) and Lowland (unmalted barley) whiskeys; and Irish whiskey, made much as Scotch is from barley, rye, oats, wheat, and other grains. Whiskey is a drink of northern Europe, where these grains readily grow, whereas the brandies, liqueurs, rum, and wines are from warmer climates, known for their fruit and sugarcane.

The *Whiskey Rebellion* is one of numerous insurrections in-volving government taxes that have occurred over the centu-ries. This particular one took place in western Pennsylvania in 1794 when the federal government, badly in need of money, tried to enforce the excise tax of 1791. It was opposed by farmers in the area who used their surplus grain to distill whiskey and culminated in riot and destruction. Before it was suppressed by the militia, a number of federal officers were tarred and feathered.

Smuggled or illicit liquor is also called *moonshine.* This term was particularly used for the product of illicit stills in the American South but apparently did not originate there. Grose's *Dictionary of the Vulgar Tongue* (1796) defines it as contrabrand liquor, specifically the white brandy smuggled on the coasts of Kent and the gin in the north of Yorkshire. Prob-ably the name was used because they were clear in color and as evanescent in appearance as moonlight. (Another theory is that the stills were operated at night, by the light of the moon.) In any event, the term surfaced again in the American South in the nineteenth century and has been associated with it ever since.

Mixed Drinks

The cocktail party has the form of friendship without the warmth and devotion. It is a device for getting rid of social obligations hurriedly en masse.
—Brooks Atkinson, *Once Around the Sun* (1951)

The term *mixed drink* has been used since about 1940 for any alcoholic drink that combines two or more ingredients, such as alcohol and fruit juice, quinine (tonic) water, soda, bitters, sugar, etc. An older name for a mixed drink is *cocktail,* whose source has been a matter of speculation for some years. About the only thing certain is that the word originated in America about 1800. There are numerous theories about its derivation, ranging from the African Creole dialect *kaktel* for "scorpion" (because the drink's "bite" is very sharp), to the Aztec princess's name *Xochitl,* who brought some cactus juice to the emperor, to the tonic invented by a New Orleans druggist, consisting of tonic and bitters and served in a *coquetier,* or egg cup. And there are at least half a dozen more equally valid ones, including those concerning mixtures fed to fighting cocks, a racehorse whose tail is "cocked," and cock tailings, liquor remnants thrown together in a large vat and sold for a song.

Whichever the true origin, the word cocktail has made its way into numerous other languages, including Russian and Japanese. Moreover, it has given rise to the *cocktail hour,* an interval preceding the evening meal during which alcoholic beverages (as well as nonalcoholic ones) are served; *cocktail napkins,* small paper or cloth napkins handed to guests with mixed drinks and the finger foods often served with them; *cocktail aprons,* frilly little aprons worn by hostesses at cocktail parties; *cocktail lounge,* a public room in a hotel, airport, restaurant, or similar place where drinks are served to customers at tables and the setting is more genteel than at a simple bar; *cocktail dress,* an elegant semiformal gown to be worn at cocktail parties and similar events; and *cocktail circuit,* a round of cocktail parties.

The word *cocktail* also has been extended to certain foods that are served as the appetizer course of a meal, such as *shrimp cocktail* or *fruit cocktail.* The allusion here is to a mixture of food and sauce or juice. On the other hand, the *Molotov cocktail* is a wholly inedible mixture. It is actually a homemade hand grenade, originally consisting of a bottle filled with inflammable liquid and fitted with either a gas-soaked rag or fuse protruding from the top. When this wick was lighted and thrown, the grenade ignited and exploded. The Molotov cocktail probably was first devised during the 1930s by Loyalists in the Spanish Civil War. But it was the Finns, using it against Russian tanks in the early 1940s, who named it for the Soviet foreign minister, Vyacheslav Mihailovich Molotov, who was a hated symbol of the Russian invaders.

> *I am prepared to believe that a dry martini slightly impairs the palate, but think what it does for the soul.*
> —Alec Waugh, *In Praise of Wine and Certain Noble Spirits* (1959)

One of the best-known mixed drinks is the *martini,* originally a mixture of gin and dry vermouth, graced with an olive or a twist of lemon peel. It dates from the late 1890s in America and probably took its name from the firm of Martini and Rossi, makers of vermouth (a fortified wine), although some authorities dispute this derivation. (In Britain the same drink is called a *gin and it.*) Although the martini's name has not been directly transferred to other items, it acquired certain connotations. It came to imply urbane sophistication (Ian Fleming's hero, James Bond, always insisted on a particular proportion of gin to vermouth and that it be stirred together rather than shaken). Also, it implies heavy drinking, for undiluted with ice it is very strong. Thus, a *three-martini lunch,* a not unusual expense-account meal for American executives in the 1950s and 1960s, implies considerable conviviality, a hard sell, and an afternoon at the office where not much of substance will be accomplished.

In Vino Veritas

Wine, my dear boy, and truth.
— Alcaeus, *Fragments* (c. 600 B.C.)

In vino veritas is the Latin version of the saying that one is bound to tell the truth after drinking enough wine, which has been a proverb since the days of ancient Greece.

Indeed, wine, the fermented juice of grapes, is one of the oldest beverages. Scientists have found evidence that grapes were a prehistoric food, and since grape juice can turn naturally into wine, it is assumed that wine was drunk in prehistoric times. Bacchus or Dionysus, the Greek god of wine, was worshiped centuries before the Christian era, and supposedly wine is mentioned some 165 times in the Bible. Among the most memorable of them is Jesus's sharing of bread and wine with his disciples at the Last Supper, the source of the Church's use of wine in the sacrament of Holy Communion.

The Greeks were the first Europeans to grow wine grapes, and they taught it to the Romans, under whom it became an important agricultural pursuit. Since then every European country whose climate is suited to viticulture (grape growing), as well as the African and Asian nations along the Mediterranean, have made wine. Probably in part because of the unhealthful character of water supplies, wine became the universal mealtime beverage in many places.

As with all crops, the yield and quality of grapes vary from year to year. A particularly good year, when wine grapes mature to perfection, is known as a *vintage year,* and the best wines are made from grapes grown in such a year. The term *vintage*—literally wine from a particular harvest or crop—has been transferred in several ways: to anything that is the best of its kind, as in, "That novel is vintage Stephen King"; to something that represents the high quality of a past era, as in, "This Rolls is a vintage automobile"; or to something that is old-fashioned and out of date, as in a "vintage hat."

> *Neither do men put new wine in old bottles: else the bottles break.*
>
> —Gospel of Matthew, 9:17

In biblical times wine was kept in wineskins made of hide or leather. New wine expands somewhat as it matures, and a new wineskin expands with it. An old one, however, can burst. The gospel quotation above alludes to this phenomenon but uses it metaphorically for any incongruity, and the expression *new wine in old bottles* continues to be so used, as well as to mean anything new put into an old framework or context.

> *O monstrous! but one half-penny worth of bread to this intolerable deal of sack!*
>
> —William Shakespeare, *Henry IV,* Part 1, 2:4

In Shakespeare's day the strong white wines imported from Spain and the Canary Islands were called *sack.* Because such wine was quite harsh-tasting, it became customary to put a piece of spiced toast into a glass of wine to improve the flavor. From this practice we have the term *drinking a toast,* that is,

DRINK AND BE MERRY 195

raising a glass of wine in honor of a particular person or event. (See also TOAST OF THE TOWN in Chapter 9.)

Wine, women, and song.
—Plutarch, *Moralia,* c. A.D. 95

The connection of wine and women was pointed out by the ancients. "There's nothing in his head but wine and women," wrote Aristophanes in *The Frogs* (405 B.C.), and numerous later writers warned that this pairing frequently caused men's downfall. Plutarch was among the earliest to add song to the combination, which centuries later became the subject of a couplet attributed to Martin Luther (it is not known who actually originated it). John Lyly had a rhymed version in *Euphues and His England* (1580): "Wine, women and song will get a man wrong." A famous waltz by Johann Strauss, Jr., is entitled *Wein, Weib, Gesang* ("Wine, Women, Song," 1869). Today the term still denotes the general merriment of drinkers, in taverns and celebrations as well as in exclusively male domains such as stag parties.

Champagne, if you are seeking the truth, is better than a lie detector.
—Graham Greene, *Travels with my Aunt* (1969)

Table wines are customarily drunk with meals. Sparkling wines, which are table wines made naturally effervescent by a second fermentation in closed containers, are usually reserved for festive occasions. The best known of them is *champagne,* which begins as a choice white table wine, usually several months old, to which yeast and sugar are added. The yeast restarts the fermentation process, and the wine is placed in bottles and corked, the cork being fastened to the bottle with a steel clamp to prevent it from blowing out. Over a period of months, the fermentation creates natural carbonic gas, which is what makes champagne bubbly. Also, carbonation causes the human body to absorb a beverage more quickly, so the effects of champagne may be felt more than is the case with a still wine, as Greene points out in the quotation above.

As might be expected, the additional processing adds to the cost of the wine, which is usually a fairly expensive one to begin with. Consequently champagne, like caviar, is associated with luxury, and used as an adjective the word has come to mean a connection with luxurious or expensive items. Thus, *champagne taste* means a taste for luxury, and the British term, *champagne socialist,* denotes an individual whose extravagant tastes and costly lifestyle do not conform to his or her declared political ideas.

Coffee Breaks

Coffee is considered the national beverage of the United States, Italy, and numerous other countries. No one knows when it was first used, but it is fairly certain that it was cultivated in Arabia by the seventh century. Prior to the fifteenth century coffee was grown exclusively in Arabia and Ethiopia. No coffee was allowed to leave those areas until after it had been roasted, so that the seed could not be planted elsewhere. It is believed that the first coffee taken to India was smuggled out of Arabia by pilgrims returning home from the holy city of Mecca, and that the Venetians were the first to bring it to Europe. Arabian coffee became known as *Mocha* for the port from which it was shipped. By the end of the seventeenth century the Dutch had introduced coffee planting in *Java.* Today the word *mocha* still signifies coffee-flavored, and *java* is a slang name for coffee itself.

Although known primarily as a nation of tea drinkers, the English opened the first *coffeehouse* in Oxford in 1650, and two years later one opened in London. Coffeehouses quickly became a social center for the wits, literati, and gossips of the day, as well as for politicians. In eighteenth-century London the Whigs were regulars at Button's Coffee House while the Tories frequented Will's Coffee House. In time *coffeehousing* came to mean chatting and gossiping, particularly when waiting for some event to begin or when putting off a job to be done. (In nineteenth-century America the latter sense was taken over in *coffee-cooler,* a now obsolete word for a loafer or shirker, and particularly for a bounty jumper, a man who joined the army for a bounty payment and then immediately left it.)

The French word for coffee, *café,* also came to mean a coffeehouse, and, when taken over into English in the late 1700s, was transferred to a small restaurant, often with an enclosed or outdoor section extending to the sidewalk. *Café* also gave rise to several other expressions taken over into English: *café au lait,* literally coffee mixed with an equal amount of hot milk, but extended to mean light brown (the color of that beverage) and also to light brown freckles, called *café au lait spots; café chantant,* literally "singing café" but referring to a small nightclub or cabaret featuring sophisticated entertainment; and, in mid-twentieth century America, *café society,* a group who habitually patronize fashionable restaurants, nightclubs, and resorts.

In America a *coffee shop* has been, since the 1830s, a small inexpensive restaurant that serves light meals. At approximately the same time, the Spanish word for coffee shop, *cafeteria,* was adopted into English, and it, too, signified a restaurant, but by the early twentieth century it was being used exclusively for a self-service restaurant.

The sociable connotations of coffee drinking were transferred in *coffee klatsch,* a term combining coffee with a German word for "noise" and denoting an informal gossip session conducted over coffee (the actual German equivalent is *Kaffeeklatsch*).

In the American workplace, a brief respite has been institutionalized in the form of the *coffee break,* which actually is specified in some labor contracts. It usually consists of ten or fifteen minutes off in mid-morning, and sometimes also in mid-afternoon, during which employees may or may not imbibe coffee. A frequent accompaniment to coffee is the doughnut, and in early twentieth-century America *coffee and* signified coffee and a doughnut or some similar snack.

Coffee is, of course, also served inside the home. Originally named for this purpose is the *coffee table,* a low table usually placed in front of a sofa and on which coffee and other drinks (it also is called a *cocktail table)* and snacks may be served. The use of the table to hold magazines and other reading matter gave rise to the term *coffee-table book,* for a book that is usually oversize, expensive, and lavishly illustrated, suitable principally for display.

Not My Cup of Tea

Whether it's served from a silver teapot at Buckingham Palace or a samovar in St. Petersburg, whether it's foamed with a bamboo whisk in Kyoto or sipped from a paper cup in Chicago, tea is a drink on which the sun never sets.
—*Consumer Reports,* July 1992

Tea, the national beverage of China, Japan, Russia, and England, has been cultivated in Asia for several thousand years. In ancient China, tea was believed to have many medicinal properties, whereas in India tea was thought to aid spiritual advancement. Tea began to be imported to Europe in the seventeenth century and very quickly attained popularity. Essays and poems were written about it, social functions began to be called *teas,* and royalty and peasants alike began to regard tea as a necessity. As a result, tea production developed into a major international industry.

In 1773 the American colonists staged the *Boston Tea Party,* dumping tea from British ships into Boston harbor in protest against British taxes. They did so at a substantial sacrifice of personal pleasure, for they then had no tea to drink until another ship arrived.

The custom of serving tea and cakes in the late afternoon, a fashion supposedly begun by Anna, Duchess of Bedford, became firmly established in Britain, and gave impetus to numerous expressions. *High tea* denotes a light early evening meal, more substantial than the afternoon tea-and-cakes repast but less so than a supper. *A nice old cup of tea* is sometimes used ironically for a messy or unpleasant situation, but when applied to a person it generally denotes a pleasant old soul. *That's another cup of tea* means that's a quite different matter, and *tea-kettle broth* signifies a poor person's meal, consisting of hot water, bread, and a small piece of butter. A *tea towel* is another name for a dish towel, and a *tea-lady* is a person who comes to the office twice a day to make tea, which is handed around at mid-morning and again at mid-afternoon (see also COFFEE BREAK).

These usages are largely British, but a number of others are current on both sides of the Atlantic. A *tea gown* is a semiformal dress worn to a mid-afternoon *tea party* and similar social occasion, which, if it features dancing, might be called a *tea dance*. While such attire is less common than in the late nineteenth century, when this term originated, it survives in *tea-length,* still applied to dresses that are slightly below mid-calf in length. *Tea and sympathy* has come to mean a sympathetic listener offering comfort to someone in distress; it gained currency in the mid-twentieth century as the title of a film (1956) starring Deborah Kerr, about a prep schoolboy's affair with a teacher's wife (based on a Broadway play of the same name by Robert Anderson).

Something that is *not my cup of tea* is clearly not to my taste. The positive version—*is my cup of tea*—dates from the late nineteenth century, and the negative from the early 1900s. From approximately the same period comes *not for all the tea in China,* not at any price. This hyperbole apparently originated in Australia and soon spread to other English-speaking countries. *A tempest in a teacup/teapot,* meaning a great to-do about not much of anything, began life as a *storm in a teacup/teapot.* It was used in that form throughout the nineteenth century, and still is in England.

The word "tea," if not the beverage, figured in another famous event in American history. In 1922 Secretary of the Interior Albert B. Fall persuaded President Warren Harding to transfer the control of naval oil reserves at Teapot Dome, Wyoming, from the Navy Department to his own department. He then leased these reserves, lands vital to the nation, to companies owned by Harry F. Sinclair and Edward L. Doheny at less than the usual rate. Moreover, later investigations showed that both men had given considerable sums to Fall, which a jury decided constituted a bribe. These events came to be known as the *Teapot Dome* scandal and helped ruin Harding's reputation.

In the early 1920s *tea* became slang for marijuana; in nineteenth-century Britain it had been, for a time, slang for any intoxicating liquor, but that usage is just about obsolete.

Making tea involves infusing dried tea leaves in hot water. Some fortune-tellers then use the wet leaves to predict the future, a practice called *reading the tea leaves*. This term has also become a synonym for fortune-telling. It is hard to say exactly when or where the practice began, but it is by no means obsolete.

Soft Drinks

We knew you had the old moxie, the old get-out-and-get.
—Max Shulman, *Barefoot Boy with Cheek* (1943)

In early twentieth-century America, Moxie was the trade name of a carbonated soft drink, somewhat bitter in flavor and extremely popular in New England. John Ciardi suggested that it may have been the Yankee love for a traditional and quite unpalatable spring tonic, sulfur and molasses, that accounted for Moxie's popularity. In fact, Moxie was invented in 1884 by Dr. Augustin Thompson, a physician from Salem, Massachusetts. At first it was marketed as a concentrated liquid, to be taken by the spoonful just before meals as a digestive aid. Its main ingredient was gentian root, and it soon was advertised as a "nerve food." By the late nineteenth century carbonated drinks were becoming popular, and Thompson decided to enter that market as well, mixing his extract with soda water. By the early 1900s Moxie was a leading soft drink, and there was even a song about it, "Just make it Moxie for mine." But the nerve-tonic idea clearly persisted, for the lower-case word *moxie* came to mean spirit, courage, and icy nerves, the last perhaps abetted by the hawker's cry of "Ice-cold Moxie" on a hot summer day.

However, Moxie never acquired the worldwide popularity of *Coca-Cola*, aided by both vigorous advertising from the time of its invention (1905) and its spread overseas by American troops during World War II. Both in America and elsewhere the name was quickly shortened to *Coke*, even though the product contained no trace of cocaine (it had originally included a minute amount). From it we have *Cocacolaization*, the unwelcome influence of American culture on European customs and institutions, a term coined in France. We also have *coke bottle*, a term applied in the mid-1950s to an airplane shape for the characteristic indentation in its middle, resembling that of the patented Coca-Cola bottle.

Drink containers of various kinds also have been linguistically transferred. The verb *to bottle up* has been applied to human emotions as well as to liquids, and *chief cook and bottle-washer* has long been used, most often sarcastically, for the principal factotum or employed helper who, often as not, gets stuck doing the boss's dirty work. And of course the *bottleneck*, for the narrowing of a passage that impedes progress, has been applied to virtually any such impediment.

A more puzzling usage is that of *fiasco*, the Italian word for "bottle," for a failure. There are numerous theories concerning it, ranging from the impossibility of a round-bottomed wine bottle to stand upright (this is true of Chianti bottles, which therefore are wrapped in straw), to the failure of an unskillful glassblower to create a bottle without breaking it. In any event, the term was first so used by the Italians themselves, who would cry "Fiasco" when an unpopular singer or actor appeared onstage, and it was taken over into English during the nineteenth century.

Not all drinks are bottled. Often they are stored in a barrel or cask, and from this we have the expression *on tap*, which at first merely meant liquor available for consumption by tapping a cask but eventually was transferred to anything or anyone ready for immediate use, as in "If John couldn't go to the Los Angeles meetings, Mary was on tap to replace him."

THIRTEEN

The Spice of Life

Variety's the very spice of life,
That gives it all its flavour.
                    —William Cowper, *The Task* (1784)

Condiments, food additives valued not for nourishment but for their flavors, have been used since ancient times. Without spices and herbs, as well as sauces made from them, food would be very dull indeed, a sentiment implicit in Cowper's poem.

In ancient times, true spices, the aromatic products of tropical plants, were known, but because they were rare and obtained with great difficulty, they were considered as valuable as gold and precious stones. Only the rich could afford them. They were offered as tribute to kings and emperors, and used in the most important religious rites. It was in hopes of finding a short passage to the Far East, the source of many spices, that Columbus undertook the voyage that brought him to America and that the sea passage around Cape Horn was discovered. Later, as one country or another tried to gain a monopoly of the *spice trade,* battles were fought and much blood was shed.

Today spices are no longer rare. Scientific methods enable most of them to be cultivated in abundance and modern dis-

tribution makes them available worldwide. Moreover, the vola-
tile oils to which spices and other natural flavorings owe their
characteristic taste often can be duplicated in the laboratory,
producing artificial flavorings that can be substituted for the
original products.

The word *spice* has been used figuratively in the sense of en-
livening or generally improving since the thirteenth century.
For example, "Hope is a swete spice" appears in the manuscript *Ancren riwle* (c. 1225), and *to spice* has been used in the
sense of "to season" almost as long.

The names of specific spices also have been transferred. An
early example, alluding to the monetary value of spices, appears in the New Testament Book of Matthew (23:23): "Ye
pay tithe of mint and anise and cummin, and have omitted . . .
judgment, mercy, and faith." Both *anise* and *cumin* seeds are
used as a spice, as are the leaves of the herb *mint*.

Ginger is a reedlike plant whose root, or rhizome, has a pungent flavor that is used in baking (see GINGERBREAD), cooking,
and such soft drinks as *ginger ale* and *ginger beer*. Its name has
been synonymous with piquancy and liveliness, and by extension with a hot temper, since the early nineteenth century. *To*

get his ginger up means to provoke someone. The pale reddish or sandy color of ground ginger also has been transferred to that shade of hair. Dickens had it in *Our Mutual Friend* (1865): "Mature young gentleman . . . with too much ginger in his whiskers."

Nutmeg, a hard seed that actually resembles a small nut, is in grated or ground form used to flavor custards, pies, cheese dishes, and eggnog. A kind of geranium is called *nutmeg geranium* because the scent of its flowers resembles the strong, musklike aroma of the spice. For the same reason a variety of muskmelon, the netted melon, is also known as *nutmeg melon.* While these transfers are quite straightforward, the use of the word for a maneuver in soccer has nothing to do with aroma. There, *to nutmeg* means to pass the ball between another player's legs and run around him or her to continue dribbling it. The player being nutmegged therefore looks very foolish. At least one authority speculates that this usage comes not from the spice but from the slang word "nuts" for testicles.

> *He taketh pepper in the nose, that I complayne upon his fautes, my selfe beyng fautless.*
>
> —John Heywood, *Proverbs* (1546)

Of all the spices, *pepper* is thought to be the one most widely used. It comes from the fruit of a perennial vine that climbs tree trunks and other supports. Native to the West Indies, it also grows in India, Sri Lanka, and Brazil. To make black pepper, the berries are picked before they are fully ripe and are dried in the sun. These black dried berries are the familiar *peppercorns.* White pepper is made from berries that ripen on the vine, where the outer hull separates from the white center. Red pepper, cayenne, and paprika comes from several species of an unrelated plant, which grows in Japan, India, Africa, Louisiana, and Hungary.

Inhaling ground pepper is apt to make one sneeze. *To take pepper in the nose,* the saying cited above, no doubt alludes to this phenomenon, and has meant to take offense since the fourteenth century. In verb form, *to pepper* means not only to sprinkle ground pepper on something but to jab repeatedly or pelt, as with shot or missiles. It also is used more figuratively, as in, "The reporters peppered the president with questions."

Probably the most common method of seasoning food, so much so that shakers of each commonly appear on Western dinner tables, are *salt and pepper.* This combination has long been transferred to a mixture of the colors white and black, as, for example, in a dark-haired person whose hair has partly turned white or gray.

A single peppercorn is not very large and hence not very valuable. In Britain, therefore, *peppercorn rent* was used in the late eighteenth century for a nominal rent and, by extension, an insignificant amount of anything. Poet William Cowper so used it in his *Table-Talk:* "His quit-rent ode, his pepper-corn of praise."

Pepper, like ginger, is pungent in flavor and so has been used in the meaning of "spirited," as in *peppery.* A mid-nineteenth-century Americanism with this meaning is the shortening *pep,* in such usages as *full of pep* or *peppy,* meaning full of vigor, and *to pep up,* or to invigorate and enliven. Athletic coaches are likely to give the team a *pep talk* in order to arouse their fighting spirit, and before a game a *pep rally* may be held to arouse the enthusiasm of both players and fans. In baseball, a *pepper game* is a pregame warmup in which a batter repeatedly bunts balls thrown by various fielders.

In the twentieth century pharmacology gave us the so-called *pep pill,* a tablet or capsule containing a stimulant drug.

With a Grain of Salt

The fact that a small amount of salt is necessary for life but that a large amount can be fatal has given salt a unique place in literature, in religious ceremonies, and in the customs of tribes and nations. To many primitive peoples, salt seemed a magic substance. The most binding pledge of loyalty from one man to another was to have *eaten his salt*. When in doubt as to the friendship of a rival king or chieftain, a medieval ruler could discover the man's intentions by offering him salt. If he ate it, all was well; it not, it was time to prepare for war. Byron described this belief in his *The Corsair:*

> *Why dost thou shun the salt? that sacred pledge*
> *Which, once partaken, blunts the sabre's edge,*
> *Makes even contending tribes in peace unite,*
> *And hated hosts seem brethren to the sight!*

In the Bible, salt is mentioned as a symbol of virtue and righteousness. Jesus told his disciples that they were *the salt of the earth* (Matthew 5:13); he meant God's chosen people, but the term still is employed for the best human beings in any context. However, when the Romans destroyed Carthage, they scattered salt on the earth where the city had been, as a symbol of its death. And the medicine men in some African tribes secretly sprinkle salt on the fields and around the huts of enemies whom they are trying to kill by means of magic spells.

Presumably it was observed early on that salt adds savor to food. A famous biblical phrase is, *If the salt have lost its savor, wherewith shall it be salted?* (Matthew 5:13; Mark 9:50; Luke 14:34), meaning if men fall from grace, how shall they be restored? From the sixteenth century on, the word *salt* also denoted strong flavor, and by extension, vigor and passion.

Shakespeare so used it, saying, "We have some salt of our youth in us" (*The Merry Wives of Windsor*, 2:3), here meaning vigor, and "Hot as monkeys, salt as wolves in pride" (*Othello*, 3:3), here meaning amorous passion. This sense of augmenting something survives in the expression *to salt an account*, meaning to raise the value of each item in it, and *to salt a mine*, introducing bits of valuable ore into a worthless mine so as to deceive prospective investors or buyers.

The value of salt also was emphasized in the medieval practice of seating honored guests *above the salt*—that is, above the point on the dinner table where a large salt cellar served as the centerpiece—and less honored ones *below the salt*. Though the practice is obsolete, the saying long survived it.

> *The captain is not worth his salt.*
> —Frederick Marryat, *The King's Own* (1830)

In Roman times soldiers were paid with *salt-money*, that is, wages with which to buy salt. In Latin this was their *salarium*, the origin of the English word "salary." From this came the expression, *(not) to be worth one's salt*, meaning to be (or not be) worth much.

To take something *with a grain of salt* also appears to have a Roman origin. In Pliny's *Natural History,* he tells of Pompey, who discovered an antidote to poison that was to be taken fasting with *addito salis grano* (the addition of a grain of salt). This became a figure of speech for accepting a statement with a certain amount of reserve, and has been so used ever since.

Yet another term originating in Rome is *Attic salt,* which means "refined wit." Cicero said, several times, that "whatever is salty and wholesome in speech is peculiar to the Attic people." The same idea was repeated by Pliny and others, who likened salt, sprinkled over food to give it a better taste, to wit, which enlivens conversation. The term was perpetuated by Milton and Byron, among others, but is heard less often today.

As pointed out at the beginning, a moderate amount of salt is necessary to sustain life of any kind, but an excess of salt destroys both animal and plant life. Meat and fish can be preserved by packing them in salt because the salt kills the bacteria that would cause spoilage. From this method of food preservation came the term *to salt away,* meaning to store anything for future use, particularly money.

A crude method of obtaining salt is by placing sea water in vessels or sand hollows and allowing the water to evaporate in the sun, leaving only the salt. The word *salt* has been used for those who love the sea, especially sailors, since the nineteenth century. A particularly experienced sailor may be called an *old salt,* which also carries the implication that he has somehow been preserved by the sea. The Indian leader Mohandas Gandhi opened his campaign for independence from British rule by making salt from sea water in defiance of the British salt tax. He explained that he chose this particular act of disobedience because salt to him was the symbol of life, and in taxing salt the British had offended against the very life of India.

To rub salt in one's wounds literally means to make them hurt considerably more, but the expression also is used figuratively to mean making an already painful matter worse. It may also be the ultimate source of *to rub something in,* meaning to emphasize an already unpleasant circumstance.

Plain Vanilla

In America vanilla, whether produced from vanilla beans, the cured pods of a tall vine native to the Americas, or an imitation extract made in the laboratory, is by far the most popular flavor of commercial ice cream. It is also widely used in making cookies, cakes, pies, puddings, and other sweet desserts. In mid-nineteenth-century Britain, its name was sometimes used figuratively to mean the very essence of a fine flavor, so that "You are the very vanilla of something" was clearly a compliment.

In late twentieth-century America, however, despite the continued popularity of vanilla flavoring, this figurative usage turned around completely. Now *vanilla* meant *plain vanilla,* that is, very ordinary and unvarnished, the garden variety, which is, by extension, dull. Thus the *plain vanilla* model of an automobile means the basic model, with no options or frills.

Piss and Vinegar

A sour liquid chemically consisting of acetic acid, vinegar can be obtained from the fermentation of wine, beer, cider, or other liquids. It has long been valued as a preservative as well as a condiment. Combined with oil it constitutes the familiar salad dressing, known by its French name, *vinaigrette.*

It is the sourness of vinegar, however, that has been linguistically transferred. Applied to people, *vinegary* denotes a crabby, ill-tempered manner or disposition. At the same time, however, *full of piss and vinegar* is a slangy Americanism for extreme exuberance and energy, not necessarily unflattering. One of America's heroes of World War II, General Joseph Stilwell, renowned for his leadership in China and Burma, was nicknamed "Vinegar Joe" Stilwell, for the sharpness of his military campaigns rather than any sourness of disposition.

Cut the Mustard

Mustard, one of the most common spices, is prepared from the seeds of the mustard plant, which is widely grown in most temperate zones of the world. To make ground mustard, the seeds are cleaned, the inner portion separated from the husks, and the meat ground fine. Prepared mustard consists of a mixture of ground mustard, vinegar, and salt and other flavorings. (Originally it was new wine, or *must,* that was mixed with the ground spice, whence its name.)

One of the oldest sayings involving mustard is *After meat, mustard,* or, as John Ray's 1670 *English Proverbs* explained, "After meat comes mustard, when there is no more use for it"— that is, something that would have been useful earlier arrives too late to be wanted at all.

Mustard is a tasty condiment but is not always benign. A common nineteenth-century remedy was the *mustard plaster,* a mixture of mustard and rubber applied to the skin as a counterirritant but often having just the opposite effect. Even more nefarious is *mustard gas,* used in chemical warfare by the Germans during World War I. An oily liquid, it irritates the skin, eyes, and lungs, sometimes causing blindness and death. It is not made from mustard but is named for its mustard-like smell.

The best-known colloquial phrase concerning mustard is *cut the mustard,* originating in America around the turn of the twentieth century. It means to come up to standard, or succeed, but its origin is a matter of dispute. Some believe it is related to the military term, "to pass muster," meaning to measure up. Others think it alludes to the preparation of mustard, in that vinegar "cuts" the bitter taste of the ground mustard seed. Most likely, however, it likens mustard, which enhances flavor, to the best or finest of something, the main attraction. Today it is most often heard in the negative, as in, "If he doesn't cut the mustard the boss will certainly fire him."

Sauces

Sauce, n. The one infallible sign of civilization and enlightenment.
—Ambrose Bierce, *The Devil's Dictionary* (1881–1906)

Like spices and condiments, sauces and gravies are flavor enhancers but in liquid form. There are many varieties, plain and fancy, ranging from commercial ketchup (or catsup), Worcestershire, and soy sauce to the most elaborate concoctions of talented chefs (the kind alluded to by Ambrose Bierce).

The English word *sauce* is ultimately derived from the Latin word for "salt," and indeed many sauces are a kind of salted seasoning. No doubt the idea of a sauce that adds piquancy to food gave rise, in the sixteenth century, to the use of *saucy* for impertinent or insolent (as in "Children must not be saucy") as well as for pert or chic ("She wore a saucy little hat"). The former meaning also exists in *saucebox,* for an impudent person, heard mostly in Britain.

It is harder to explain the use of *the sauce* for liquor, a slang usage originating in America in the 1930s. Nevertheless, to be *on the sauce* means to be drinking, usually with the implication of overindulgence.

The Spanish word for sauce, *salsa,* today has been partially adopted into English for a spicy, peppery sauce associated with Mexican and other Latin American cookery. In the 1970s it acquired yet another meaning, that of Latin American dance music incorporating elements of several important dances, notably the mambo and the cha cha cha.

> *I don't get a damn penny of town money, so everything I do for you's gravy, and you treat me like I'm delivering pizza.*
> —Jeffery Wilds Deaver,
>   *The Lesson of Her Death* (1993)

"Sauce" can be a sweet or sour or salty liquid—for example, chocolate sauce poured over ice cream, hollandaise sauce served with fish, bordelaise (a red-wine sauce) served with beef, and many other concoctions. The word *gravy* is more specific, that is, a sauce made from the juices and fat that exude from cooking meat. Whether or not embellished with other flavorings or thickened with flour, gravy is always savory rather than sweet, and is served with meat and accompanying vegetables. Soon after 1900, *gravy* became an American slang word for money, especially an extra sum obtained without much effort, an unexpected windfall. Presumably the analogy is to the meat juices constituting gravy, which effortlessly drip during the cooking process. In the 1920s the term was lengthened to *gravy train,* which signified a job or position associated with extra money or advantages but no work or effort. It is still so used, as in, "Despite a shrinking school population, automatic tenure and annual salary increases put these school administrators on the gravy train."

FOURTEEN

What's Cooking?

The fact that *too many cooks spoil the broth* has long been known, and its transfer to any enterprise in which too many participants hamper its success was already proverbial by 1575. Of much more recent provenance is *What's cooking?*—a slangy Americanism of the late 1930s that transfers what's going on in the kitchen to what's happening just about anywhere. The slightly newer (1940s) expression *(now you're) cooking with gas* signifies rapid progress; it presumably compares the rapidity of cooking on a gas range to more primitive and slower methods. Slightly later variations, such as *cooking with electricity* or *radar*, have not survived. But President Harry Truman's dictum, *"If you can't stand the heat, get out of the kitchen,"* has long outlasted its inventor with no change of meaning, that is, if you can't stand the pace/stress/problems of this situation, don't become involved.

Most kitchen stoves have at least four burners, and cooks tend to put the slowest-cooking items toward the back and the fastest, and those that need more frequent stirring or other at-

tention, toward the front. From this practice American government officials transferred the terms to low- and high-priority concerns—the low-priority being put on a *back burner* and important ones, requiring immediate attention, on a *front burner.* The former dates from about 1960, and the latter, which never caught on to as great an extent, from the early 1970s.

Cooking and Baking

Cooking is, of course, a perfectly honorable term for preparing food by subjecting it to heat. To *cook up* something, however, means to concoct a plan, and often it implies some measure of deceit or deception (as in, "She cooked up yet another excuse for cutting classes"). And *cooking the books* signifies outright dishonesty, since it means falsifying financial records in order to deceive stockholders, conceal theft, avoid taxes, or some other nefarious purpose. (For cooking someone's goose, see GOOSE.)

A number of cooking techniques have been transferred. In Britain, to give someone *a basting* means to give him or her a beating; Ebenezer Brewer speculates that it comes from the long-handled wooden spoon used to baste meat on a turnspit, which an irate cook might turn on a lazy helper. In any event, this usage is less common in America.

Boiling has given rise to a number of widely used expressions. Food that reaches the boiling point bubbles and churns, a characteristic soon transferred to human anger in such expressions as *boiling mad,* or *boiling with rage,* or *reaching the boiling point.* In contrast, the bubbling action has been transferred to very positive feelings, as in *bubbling over with joy/excitement/ anticipation,* all meaning to experience these feelings in a sparkling, effervescent way. As anyone who has ever boiled water knows, if it boils long enough it evaporates, reducing the quantity of whatever is in the pot (or worse yet, burning the food and/or the pot). From this comes the verb *to boil down to,* meaning to reduce something to its essence. Finally, an egg boiled for three or four minutes remains soft (and is said to be soft-boiled). Allowed to remain in boiling water for ten minutes or more, both white and yolk solidify completely, earning it the name *hard-boiled.* By the late nineteenth century this term was being applied to hardheaded, shrewd, unsentimental individuals, by Mark Twain among others, and it continues to be so used.

> *Are bean claims half-baked?*
> —Alysia Tate, *Boston Globe,* July 10, 1993

Bread or other food that is *half-baked* is obviously underdone. Logically enough the term was transferred to persons or enterprises that are somehow incomplete, or crude, or unfinished, as long ago as the early seventeenth century. The *Globe* reporter quoted above was writing about the state's "standard of identity" regulation for baked beans, which in Massachusetts is an issue of tradition rather than nutrition (or logic; also see BEANTOWN in Chapter 2).

The exact opposite of half-baked is meant by *done to a turn* (also put as *roasted to a turn),* which originally referred to meat being turned on a spit to the precisely right degree of doneness. The term occasionally is transferred to some undertaking that has been very satisfactorily completed.

Roasting meat is an old and perfectly legitimate method of preparation. However, in medieval times, when torture was an accepted commonplace, the verb *to roast* meant to torture someone with exposure to extreme heat. Presumably from this singularly unpleasant practice comes a more recent transfer, that is, *to roast* meaning to expose someone to the more figurative pain of cruel banter or criticism. And in modern times, *a roast* can refer to a banquet or similar occasion at which one or more guests of honor are made fun of in a more (or less) good-humored fashion. Such an occasion is also called a *celebrity roast.*

Stew in Your Own Juice!

They may stew in their own juice.
—S. J. Weyman, *Shrewsbury* (1898)

Stewing is yet another time-honored cooking method whose name has been transferred. Slow boiling or simmering for several hours can make a delectable dish, usually consisting of a mixture of meat and vegetables. The verb *to stew,* however, also came to mean an emotional version of a slow boiling—that is, the process of worrying or fretting or being agitated over a period of time. It also is put as being *in a stew.* And *to stew in one's own juice* has meant, since the late 1800s, to suffer the consequences of one's own actions. A much earlier version of this turn of phrase is *to fry in one's own grease,* a locution used by Chaucer in *The Wife of Bath's Prologue* (1386) and frequently repeated for several hundred years but heard less often today.

According to Nelson Algren's book, *America Eats,* "stew" was the name of a beverage popular with early Illinois settlers. It resembled a hot toddy, containing whiskey, water, sugar, spices, and butter. The last day of school customarily was celebrated with a party, at which the schoolmaster occasionally overindulged in this stew. From this, Algren believed, came the expression *to be stewed,* still one of many slang terms for being intoxicated.

Although many regard stew as an absolutely delicious repast, it formerly was considered a dish far inferior to a large roast, for into the stew pot went small, leftover scraps of meat and vegetables. Consequently, *going to pot* came to mean being ruined or destroyed. John Heywood's proverb collection of 1546 had, "The weaker goeth to the potte," and the idea of ruin was well established by the end of the sixteenth century.

Nevertheless, just about every nation has developed its own version of stew, with characteristic ingredients. Thus *Irish stew* traditionally is thick with potatoes; New England's *oyster stew* is a creamy seafood delicacy; the Spanish *olla podrida* (literally "rotten pot") is highly seasoned; the French have their *pot au feu* (formerly called *potpourri),* the Scots their *hotch potch* or *hodgepodge* ("pot of hashed-up food"), the Italians *salmagundi,* the Hungarians their paprika-flavored *goulash,* and so on. Many of these originally foreign names have been taken over into English and then transferred to signify any mixture or miscellaneous collection. Sometimes further refinements develop. In the late 1980s British journalists called Hungary's brand of communism, which included elements of capitalism, *goulash communism.* This particular neologism has died out, however, owing to subsequent political changes.

Pots and Pans

Frying-Pan, n. One part of the penal apparatus employed in that punitive institution, a woman's kitchen. The frying-pan was invented by Calvin. . . .
—Ambrose Bierce, *The Devil's Dictionary* (1881–1906)

A trout about to be fried is not in a very happy condition, and if in the course of cooking it should fall from the pan into the fire, the situation is obviously bad for both fish and cook. The proverb *Out of the frying pan into the fire* was already familiar in the early sixteenth century and appears in many languages; in all of them, it means going from bad to much worse.

Another hazard of cooking over an open fire, observed just as long ago, is that it flares up when grease drips into it. This circumstance, too, found its way into proverb collections, as *(now) the fat's in the fire,* meaning now the damage has been done.

A watched pot never boils, they say—only this one finally did.
—Clare Boothe, *Europe in the Spring* (1940)

The word "pot" for a cooking vessel has been around for nearly a thousand years, and has spawned numerous proverbs. From the days of cooking over open fires comes *the pot calls the kettle black.* Versions of it date from the sixteenth century. All of them mean, as the saying still does, accusing someone of faults that one has oneself, alluding to the fact that an open fire tends to blacken all cooking utensils equally.

The hyperbole that *a watched pot never boils*—that is, eagerly awaiting an event makes it seem extremely slow to arrive—is of later provenance, first appearing in print in the mid-nineteenth century, but the observation is surely much older.

The expression *to keep the pot boiling* long meant to earn money so as to keep food in the house; it first appeared in the sixteenth century but is seldom heard in this form today. However, it survives in the word *potboiler,* coined in the mid-nineteenth century for a work of art or literature of mediocre quality that is produced entirely for financial gain. Critics frequently take a *potshot* at such works, that is, they subject them to random criticism. Originally a potshot was a shot fired at game so as to obtain food for the pot, without using particular skill or observing any rules of sportsmanship. The term originated in the second half of the nineteenth century and was being used figuratively a few decades later.

Also still current is the much older *(to take) potluck,* which appeared in print in 1592 (in a letter of Thomas Nashe's). It was used then, and still is, for a guest who takes his or her chances as to what might be served at a meal (that is, what happens to be in the pot). Today it also signifies a meal to which each guest contributes all or part of a course, with a similar result: no one knows just what will be served.

The traditional pot's rounded shape is alluded to in the term *potbelly,* for any rounded, protuberant midsection. Alexander Pope may have been the first to use it for a human being in the early eighteenth century and it is still so used. It also is applied to the wood- or coal-burning *potbelly stove,* no longer as common a household item. For FLESHPOT, see Chapter 8.

Another kitchen item whose shape has been transferred is the *panhandle.* Especially when cooking over an open fire, a long handle makes a frying pan both easier and safer to manipulate. In mid-nineteenth-century America this term began to be applied to a long, narrow strip of land that projects from a larger, broader area. Such areas are found in Texas *(Texas Panhandle)*, Idaho, Alaska, Florida, Oklahoma, and West Virginia, the last of which is nicknamed the *Panhandle State.* The beggar seeking a handout with arm outstretched gave rise to the term *panhandler.*

Tableware

Eating meals while seated at a table is a relatively recent refinement, dating back only a few hundred years. Nevertheless, the utensils used in this enterprise have also been linguistically transferred.

Born with a Silver Spoon

Not every man is born with a *silver spoon* in his mouth, a saying that dates from the early seventeenth century and continues to be repeated, equating this utensil with being fortunate enough to inherit wealth.

Whether made of silver or some baser metal or wood, this useful utensil has found its way into numerous locutions. To be *spoon-fed* has signified being treated like a baby—pampered, but also not given the chance to think for oneself—since about 1900. In contrast, *he needs a long spoon who sups with the devil,* an adage dating from the time of Chaucer (who may have originated it in his *The Squire's Tale),* warns that one will need to take great care (keep one's distance) in any alliance with evil.

The verb *to spoon* not only means to transfer food by means of this utensil but to make love in a sentimental fashion, also called *spooning.* One writer believes this term came from the Welsh practice of presenting one's lady love with an elaborately carved wooden spoon. Ebenezer Brewer believed it came from a now seldom used meaning of *spoon*—that is, a simpleton or fool, which was extended to foolish lovemaking. The true origin is not clear, but the usage became current in the mid-nineteenth century and is, in an era of more explicit sexual expression, obsolescent if not obsolete.

The spoon's rounded, concave shape has caused the word to be transferred to other, similarly shaped objects—a fish lure, a Number 3 wooden golf club, a surgical instrument, a *spoon-back chair*. A soft cornmeal mixture of the American South is called *spoon bread* because it can be served (and eaten) with a spoon; the same name is also used for biscuits shaped by dropping the batter from a spoon.

Finally, a *greasy spoon* has been American slang for a cheap and not very clean restaurant since about 1910 and continues to conjure up a graphic image of unsanitary practices.

Knife and Fork

Although the *fork* is undeniably useful at the table, it began life in much larger form on the farm, used to manipulate hay, for digging (a spading fork), and similar tasks. In Roman times the word (*furca* in Latin) also meant a kind of yoke to which prisoners were tied (and then tortured), as well as the gallows. It was only in the fifteenth century that forks began to be used in the kitchen and at the table. Owing to the fork

prongs' resemblance to fingers, *fork* became underworld slang for the fingers, and by extension for a pickpocket. From this came the usage *to fork out,* meaning to hand over something (usually money).

Since the *knife* is a cutting instrument with far older and wider uses than simply cutting food, it is in most cases impossible to determine what kind of knife has been transferred in such terms as *knife edge.* One expression, however, is undoubtedly from the table knife: the term *knife and fork,* used literally to mean eating, and in such phrases as "He is a good knife-and-fork," meaning he is a hearty eater. It dates from the eighteenth century.

> *He looked at me as if I was a side dish he hadn't ordered.*
> —Ring Lardner (1885–1933), quoted as
> alluding to President William Howard Taft

The word *dish* can mean either a container for food or the food itself. In mid-twentieth-century American slang, the noun *dish* signified a singularly attractive woman, a usage falling into disuse. Further, the word is also a verb, as in *to dish out,* meaning to serve food or, by extension, to distribute something else. The slangy *to dish it out,* however, means to dispense abuse, or flattery, or other verbiage, in copious quantities. In nineteenth-century Britain the intransitive verb had still another meaning, that is, *to be dished (up)* meant to be done for, and *to be dished out of (something)* meant to be cheated out of it.

A flat sort of dish is a *plate,* whose name in fact comes from the Latin word for "flat." *To have a lot/enough on one's plate* transfers a plate filled with food to a full agenda, a usage dating from the 1920s. Similar analogies have been drawn to other utensils, the most familiar, perhaps, being *My cup runneth over* (Psalm 23:5), here referring to an embarrassment of riches.

Free Lunches and Meal Tickets

There's no such thing as a free lunch.

The American economist Milton Friedman frequently used the phrase above in the 1970s in order to support his theory of monetarism, but he did not originate it. Rather, it dates from the mid-nineteenth century, when saloons would try to attract customers by offering "free" food to accompany their drinks. Presumably the prices of drinks were jacked up to cover the food cost, and those who tried to get away with eating but ordered no drinks would be told, "No free lunch here." According to sociologist Irving Lewis Allen, initially the better establishments put up high-quality food for their "free lunch." This practice was also adopted by disreputable saloons, although their fare was far from appetizing, and a common fork, kept in a glass of water, was shared by all the customers. After about 1910 the free lunch was largely abandoned, at least in New York City, owing to new laws governing licensing and sanitation. Nevertheless, the term is still used, and not only by economists, to indicate that you can't get something for nothing, and in one way or another you must pay for anything you get.

In the second half of the twentieth century there arose the term *power lunch,* that is, a meal at which business executives made deals, tried to impress their luncheon companions, or simply appeared in order to be seen. Raymond Sokolov described a New York restaurant often used for such occasions as "the Mount Whitney of lunches" and a strategically placed corner table there as "the holy of holies" (*Wall Street Journal,* June 20, 1984).

Square meals, not adventurous ones, are what you should seek.
—Bryan Miller, *New York Times,* Sept. 26, 1986

The term *square meal,* for a substantial and nourishing one, originated in mid-nineteenth-century America. The "square" here means full or complete. Presumably such a meal would consist of numerous *courses,* a word sometimes transferred to various stages of some other enterprise. The names of courses can be similarly transferred—for example, "The overture served as an *appetizer* for the long program."

In late nineteenth-century America it was sometimes the practice to give out *meal tickets,* that is, tickets that entitled their holders to a meal. In the early twentieth century this term was transferred to any individual or circumstance that ensured either income or success. In sports, for example, it was applied to a consistently good player who could be counted on to help the team to win. Thus Carl Hubbell of the New York Giants was dubbed "King Carl the Meal Ticket," and in the early 1990s the same sobriquet might well be attached to basketball's Michael Jordan of the Chicago Bulls.

Dinner in the diner, Nothing could be finer
Than to have your ham and eggs in Carolina.
—Mack Gordon, "Chattanooga Choo Choo" (1941)

The word *diner* means, of course, a person who is eating dinner. However, in the heyday of American railroading, it also was an abbreviation for the *dining car,* where one could consume a sumptuous meal in comparative elegance. When a railroad dining car had outlived its usefulness, it sometimes was bought by an eager restaurateur who converted it into an inexpensive short-order establishment, usually located near the railroad station where it had been left.

Irving Lewis Allen, in his *The City in Slang,* described another source. In the 1890s New York and other large eastern cities replaced most of their old horse-drawn streetcars with electric trolleys. Restaurateurs bought the discarded streetcars very cheaply and converted them into stationary lunch cars. At first they had only counters with bar stools, which women in their long skirts found awkward. Nevertheless, the success of these enterprises soon spurred the manufacture of large, shiny lunch cars with booths to seat the ladies and their families. They were modeled after the original railroad dining cars and, by 1900 or so, were, in further imitation, called *diners.*

The elegance of the diner, whether created from actual railroad cars or simply in imitation of them, did not survive in either ambiance or food, so that, as John Ciardi pointed out, they became synonymous with such slangy names as *greasy spoon* (see also above), *ptomaine palace,* or *hash house.* Today they have been largely replaced by fast-food chains, which offer mass-produced, standardized food and specialize in quick but minimal service, but a few diners still survive.

> *I personally prefer a nice frozen TV dinner at home because it's so little trouble. All you have to do is have another drink while you're throwing it in the garbage.*
> —Jack Douglas, *Never Trust a Naked Bus Driver* (1960)

Probably nothing has been so reviled by gourmets as the *TV dinner,* unless it is airline food, which is so closely related as to be indistinguishable from it. Originating about 1950, it consists of a quick-frozen meal (typically meat, potatoes, vegetables) which can be heated in its own tray and presumably consumed in front of a television set (whence the name) so that the viewer suffers little program interruption in preparing it.

The words *gourmand* and *gourmet* both have been taken over directly into English from French. The former, used in English from the fifteenth century on, still means "glutton," and the latter, adopted in the early nineteenth century, means "epicure." Both are occasionally transferred, the one to other kinds of greediness and the other to connoisseurship.

Gourmets are known for their love of *tidbits,* that is, choice morsels of food. This term, too, has been widely transferred to other small bits and pieces, particularly items of gossip. Actually, the relation between eating and talking is essentially logical in that both are oral activities. Hence we have such common phrases as *You said a mouthful* and *Don't put words in my mouth,* as well as *He is going to eat his words.*

We are what we eat, as that brilliant French gastronomist Anthelme Brillat-Savarin first put it in 1825 *(La physiologie du goût),* so let us end with *Bon appétit!*

INDEX